A Bridge to Healing: J.T.'s Story
Companion Workbook

A Guide to Connecting to the Other Side

Sarina Baptista

ISBN: 978-0-9912552-0-7 (sc)
ISBN: 978-0-9912552-1-4 (e)

Bridge to Healing books may be ordered through booksellers or by contacting:

Bridge to Healing Press
1966 W. 15th Street, Suite 4
Loveland, CO 80538
(970) 290-9236
www.bridgetohealing.com

Because of the dynamic nature of the Internet, any web addresses or links contained in this book may have changed since publication and may no longer be valid.

The author of this book does not dispense medical advice or prescribe the use of any technique as a form of treatment for physical, emotional, or medical problems without the advice of a physician, either directly or indirectly. The intent of the author is only to offer information of a general nature to help you in your quest for emotional and spiritual wellbeing. In the event you use any of the information in this book for yourself, which is your constitutional right, the author and the publisher assume no responsibility for your actions.

Printed in the United States of America

Cover design by Sarina Baptista
Cover photography by Sarina Baptista
Bridge to Healing Press rev. date: 12/18/2013

For my amazing family, John, J.T., Lacey and Anthony. You have been on this crazy ride with me, and have never lost faith in who we are and where we are going. Thank you!

Table of Contents

Preface

I was a stay at home mom of three beautiful children in 2007. They were seven, five and three. Needless to say, I was busy and allowed life to take on a pace of its own. I knew how blessed I was, though. We had a close call with my youngest when he was born. I realized when he was in open heart surgery at eight days old that life was very fragile.

The day we took him home from the hospital, another baby was admitted to the same NICU. Of all the beds in that 50 bed NICU, our boys were placed side by side. This little one belonged to close family friends. We spent all our holidays together since I married my husband. I felt so awkward showing them the "ropes" of the NICU, while we were waiting for our son to be discharged.

Their baby didn't make it. I knew so clearly that it could have gone either way—it could have been our baby we were burying instead of theirs.

Fast forward three years. Our little cardiac baby is thriving and is now three years old. We are driving in my husband's truck on a beautiful March Saturday. We are on the way home from the store where we bought the *20 Greatest Hits* CD by Chris LeDoux. Everyone in the car is singing "Life Is A Highway" at the top of their lungs. In that moment, I said to myself, "It doesn't get any better than this" and I just drank it in.

Two days later, my oldest, J.T., and his sister, Lacey, catch the flu. They are both very sick, but Lacey is vomiting and has a much higher fever than J.T. My week is dedicated to attending to my babes, making sure they have water and nourishment. Neither improves by Thursday, when I get food poisoning. I am in bed the entire day. At 11pm, my fever breaks and I get an unusual surge of energy. I check on my sickies. Lacey is asleep, but J.T. is having one heck of a time getting comfortable. His breathing is affected by the virus, so we try different things…having him sit in the bathroom with a hot shower running, driving in the cool night air, back rubs, vaporizers, expectorants. Nothing is helping, though. I thought about taking him to the emergency room, but a part of me said no, that wouldn't help at all. The only energy I have from being sick all day is to stay conscious for J.T. and help him in any way I can. About 3:30am, while I lie in the bed next to him, he pops up in bed and says, "Mommy, go to your room." I was half asleep and asked him if he wanted to come with me. He said, no, he wanted to watch TV. I replied "OK," not really thinking about how out of character this was for my mama's boy, only seven years old at the time. I got up, turned on his TV and went across the hall to my room.

At 6am I went to the bathroom. I paused before going back to bed and thought I should check on J.T. "*What if he's gone?*" Why would I think such a thing? He has the flu, that's all.

I went to his door and saw him peaceful on his bed.

"*Thank God, he finally got to sleep.*" Then I noticed his chest was not moving. My son was not breathing.

Paramedics, police, ambulance...it was a blur from there. I managed to drive to the hospital on my own. My husband had to find someone to watch Lacey and Anthony before he could join me. The moment the doctor came into the "family" room next to the ER and said, "We lost him," my world shattered and my heart was broken beyond repair.

Or so I thought. I had no idea what J.T. was planning for me in his current state of energy. I could not have dreamed that over the next six years how my life, once destroyed, could be restored piece by piece by an orchestra of helpers I could not even see.

Even before I learned what I know now to be my truth, I knew there was some force helping me – helping me get up in the morning and tend to my heartbroken children, helping me move through my own grief, helping me out of the grief pit when I felt I would not be able to survive. I could almost feel the hand of God reaching down and helping me up out of the abyss when I really just wanted to die. I did not know that from this pain could come something so amazing and indescribable. I would find my "why" – Why am I here? Why did my son die? Why does anyone have to go through this?

In October 2007, I discovered I could hear my son from the other side. I could also hear other people's children, and my angels and guides. Six short months after burying my son, I had proof my son was still "alive." He was not the kind of "alive" I wanted him to be, but I would take what I could get! I trained and practiced, meditated, practiced more, did everything I needed to do to hone that connection with my son. I learned what worked for me, what didn't, and how to raise my vibration to hear him clearer. I learned to train my other senses so that I could hear, see, feel and know what my angels, guides and J.T. were communicating to me.

A month later, I started to receive messages from more kids on the other side, who wanted so desperately to let their parents know they were okay. A year later, I began my own meditation group and in January 2009, I began to train others to communicate with the other side. I need to correct that last statement— I did not begin to train others. My guides did. I remember when they told me I needed to start a mentorship program and teach others what I learned thus far, I laughed, "I'm not qualified!" They told me, "Sarina, you don't need to be qualified to teach them, because you won't be doing the teaching. We will." It was quite a shift to rely solely on teachers I couldn't touch in the flesh, but boy, were they effective! As long as I stayed out of the way and facilitated their training, my teaching guides knew what each individual needed to hone his or her gifts quickly and efficiently. All I had to do was be the interpreter.

I am six years down this path and I remain amazed at the ease and simplicity in training others to tune into their innate abilities to receive messages from Spirit. This workbook is the culmination of what my teaching guides have given me and the students in my psychic/mediumship training program. It is the foundation upon which you can build any kind of connection to any kind of energy—human, animal, angel, multi-dimensional—you name it.

We are all psychic, and we receive information from our angels, guides and loved ones. All the time. How you tune into this communication and filter it determines your clarity and how well you receive information. I know beyond a shadow of a doubt, that if I can connect clearly to the other side, anyone can.

Stay-At-Home-Mom turned Psychic-Medium-Author-Trainer. Yes, you can do this, too! Believe it. Know it. And most of all, do it. You will be so amazed at who you are and who you will become. Enjoy the journey!

Introduction: How to Navigate This Workbook

Congratulations on choosing to connect with your angels, guides and loved ones and making the commitment to learn (or re-learn) this invaluable skill. We can all connect and receive clearly. Over the next twenty four weeks, you will be instructed on how you can hone your innate gifts. Before getting started, there are some basics we need to cover.

You may have downloaded this workbook from an electronic source. My teaching guides gave me the instruction to put this in electronic format for ease of use. They wanted this workbook to be available to you wherever you are. Because this is a workbook, you will need to keep a separate notebook/journal for responses to the questions and exercises. Another option is to add your notes with your e-reader if it has that capability. Whichever method works for you, be sure to have access to this workbook wherever you go so you can take full advantage of special moments you have with Spirit.

This workbook is broken into weekly lessons. There are twenty-four lessons in all, which is about six months of work. The exercises and questions are in block format so you can identify what it is you need to do. You may find you have to take a break from the work due to life issues and events. Please do not feel you have to finish this workbook in the six month timeframe. Do what is right for you. If you find you need more than one week for a lesson, by all means, carry the exercises into the next week. This is *your* training. Do what you need to do to be successful.

If you have read A Bridge to Healing: J.T.'s Story, this first month's exercises might be review for you. We are building the foundation for the rest of the course. Do the exercises anyway, even if you feel you have done them before.

I encourage you to take the full week to complete the lesson. Faster is not better. This workbook is created by my High Teaching Guides to foster the most success for you. Rushing through the lessons does not give your spirit and psyche the time to process what you are learning.

If at any time during your training you want validation for your experiences or a little more individualized instruction, I offer a discounted consultation rate (20% off) for anyone using this workbook. Please visit my website at http://www.sarinabaptista.com. There you will find my current rates and can contact me for a consultation. Be sure to make a note when you schedule the appointment that you have the workbook so I apply the proper credit.

Above all else, have fun and enjoy this process! Should you get frustrated because it isn't working the way you think it should, take a break! Remember, "If Sarina can do this, I surely can do this!" I am not special. I had an extraordinary circumstance pushing me into this arena and the necessity to learn how to communicate with my son on the other side. Regardless of where you are on your path or what is propelling you to make this connection, know you can do it. You would not believe how many helpers are waiting to assist you. They help you every day. Wouldn't it be wonderful to have that two way communication with them? Get ready! This is the beginning of that amazing connection!

Part One: Definitions and Explanations

Energy 101

I want to take time to demystify what I do. I tune into energies. These energies could be your loved ones, or they could be your body's energies, depending on what type of session I am doing. In a mediumship session, I am asking for that loved one's energy to come close and communicate. In a psychic session, I am tuning into my client's energy to see what he or she might need to do to get on path. Both types of sessions are done in the same manner; I tune into the vibration of the energy.

Everything in the Universe is energy. We were energy before we came into these bodies, we are energy in these bodies, and we will be energy when we leave these bodies. One of the most basic laws of science is the Law of the Conservation of Energy. Energy cannot be created or destroyed; it can only be changed from one form to another.

All energy also has a vibration, the "energetic signature." The vibration is the frequency and velocity of the energy. Even trees have a vibration. By tuning into the particular way in which that energy vibrates, or its energetic signature, I can receive information from it and about it.

What does this mean for you? It means you can learn to tune in and receive by learning about energy. The way we communicate with our loved ones, angels and guides is through vibration. In this book, you will learn to identify the spirit with whom you are connecting through its vibration. Right now, let's do an exercise to show you your own vibration.

Hands Exercise

> Sit with your feet flat on the floor and your
> back straight, hands palms down in your lap.
> Take your hands and put them chest high,
> palms facing each other about two feet apart.
> Slowly, move your hands together until the
> almost touch, leaving about an inch between

them. Hold them there. What do you notice is happening between your hands?
Next, slowly pull your hands away from each other. What do you notice now?
Then, move both your hands to the top of your head, palms touching your head. What do you feel on the top of your head?
What was your experience when your hands were far apart?
What happened when you moved the together and then apart again?
What happened when you then put your hand on your head?

This exercise demonstrates how your energy flows and vibrates! You are an energetic being, and so are your loved ones, angels and guides!

How Do I Know I Have the Right Loved One?

The first thing I do when I sense an energy is determine its qualities. The questions I ask are "Is it male or female?" and "Is it vibrating at a fast rate or a slow rate?"

Based upon these answers, I further determine what relation this energy has to my client—father, mother, sister, brother, child, etc.

The next step is to have the energy use whatever means necessary to communicate more specific information. I receive information through seeing, feeling, knowing and hearing. Many energies prefer to use pictures to show me who they are or give me information specific to their loved one. Many like to talk to me, giving me the inflection of their voice or the characteristics of who they are by the way they speak. Others communicate through my physical body, or feeling, giving me impressions of how they felt physically before they passed. Some energies are very good communicators and some are not. Maybe they were shy when they were here, so they behave shyly and stay in the back of the room. Possibly, they might feel responsible for how they passed, so they will not come close, which makes clear communication more challenging.

When this occurs, I ask my guides to intervene and interpret for the energy so we can still receive the validation. We have to remember these are still "people." They just don't have their bodies anymore. It seems more often than not, once I ask my guides to intervene and we find why they are staying away, they feel comfortable and move closer to me.

Only once do I remember such difficulty in the communication that I did not feel comfortable with what the energy was telling me. She was the daughter of a person I knew, and she almost seemed bothered I would ask her to come. Her mother wanted specific answers to specific questions, and the daughter I could see just rolled her eyes. She would say to me, "This is the most important thing my mom wants to know about me now?" It is very important to your loved ones that you receive what they want to give to you instead of *demanding* specific information from them to prove themselves. The connection will get fuzzy and the loved one may stop communicating altogether. My client's daughter taught me much about the other side and about communication, as frustrating as it was at the time!

I bring up this particular instance because it is natural for us to want to receive specific information from our loved ones, something that would surely, beyond a shadow of doubt, identify them. I have learned it is up to our loved ones as to what they want to communicate, not us. Keep a very open mind and receive what they tell you. Putting limitations on the communication just leaves you frustrated and doubting. Part of this journey is to weed through the doubt and believe what you are receiving. Our loved ones will always give us something to identify who they are. Be open to what they give you. It will make the connection much easier.

Terms and Definitions

Before we study how to receive information, we first need to learn some of the vernacular.

Psychic

A psychic can read energy from a person, place or thing and receives information based upon that energy. He or she can look into the past, present or future of that energy to see what might help that energy reach its highest potential. The psychic may or may not be able to connect with your deceased loved ones.

Medium

A medium is a person who can communicate with your deceased loved ones, your angels and your guides.

Psychic Medium

A psychic medium can connect with your loved ones, angels and guides, as well as read energy.

Spirit

A spirit can refer to any energy that does not have physical form. Of course, we all have a spirit, or soul, within us, that is not limited to the confines of our body. It is an independent energy.

Ghost

A ghost is the energy of an animal or person previously in physical form. When the body dies, the spirit leaves the body and goes into an energy space very close to the one in which we live. From there, the spirit can decide to continue their journey and move into even higher energy spaces (heaven or higher dimensions) or stay where they are. When a spirit stays where they are, they are considered a ghost because they can manifest their presence to those still in bodies. The process of moving into the higher spaces varies from soul to soul and can take anywhere from two months to a year or more, depending on that soul's life here and the choices he or she made.

Crossed Over

We say a spirit has "crossed over" when that spirit has decided to go to the higher energy spaces.

High Vibration vs. Low Vibration

A high vibration is someone who has crossed over and sees the bigger picture. A low vibration is an energy that has chosen to stay at the same vibrational level as when he or she "died." A low vibration does not see the bigger picture and is usually not trustworthy as a communicator. Many low vibrations believe they know what is best for us, but until they raise their vibration to see the bigger picture for them and us, they don't.

It is important to determine if an energy with which you are communicating is high or low in vibration. This will tell you whether the information is accurate and for your highest good.

When we first leave our bodies, we do not see the big picture yet. I find conversing with those recently departed is more like a conversation I would have with them when they were alive—there is still an ego attachment and a lot of emotion about what they did with their lives and the mistakes they made, or the mistakes others made against them. They do not see how it all fits into a plan and how they were part of that plan.

This is very important to remember since we still have the emotional attachments to our loved ones. If a loved one comes through and has any emotional response to questions, I know they have not been gone very long. I also know to take the information they give me with a grain of salt because, again, they are not seeing the picture from the higher perspective.

As time passes after we leave our bodies, our vibration gets higher and we can see the bigger picture. We learn more about who we are as spirits and how we are to help those still on Earth. We understand the role we had in their lessons and the role they had in helping us learn our own lessons. We shed the hang ups, the attitudes, the disagreements and all emotion attached to what happened in our lives. We keep the love and the deepness of the relationships, especially with our families. We understand why we chose the mother and father we did in that life, and why our children are who they are. There is no sense of time in the spirit world, so this may take a few months to a few years, or longer, in Earth terms. There is no pressure to get it done, but we are gently encouraged by our loved ones and guides to do the work.

I want to be clear here because if you have lost a child, you worry about where he or she is. Children are never alone and seem to adapt back into the Spirit world much faster than adults. Their mission will be to help you through your process, whatever that may entail. They work very diligently to get you those signs and try to communicate through dreams, songs, animals and whatever other means they can.

The other circumstance about which parents worry is when their child left by their own choice and doing, such as suicide and overdose. I have communicated with many of these children. In fact, my first contact with a child other than J.T., of course, was Zane who left by suicide. These spirits might take a little longer raising their vibration, but I always hear they are exactly where they need to be. This means they are doing their work and learning about how their choice affected the plan and what they need to do to balance that energy. There are usually angels surrounding these souls and helping them assimilate back into the Spirit world. It is possible they need to isolate themselves for a time. They are always available to talk to their parents, though, so please do not worry about contacting them. They will be there waiting for you.

Those who have had a particularly difficult and painful life here on Earth might also choose to isolate for a time since that lifetime took its toll on the soul. Again, this is normal and there are no time constraints on when they need to reemerge. These souls might feel a bit farther away when we communicate with them, but again, they are always accessible.

Sometimes when people feel they have not led a good life or they have done things they should not have done, they are fearful of being sent to "hell." They will not go into the light or "cross-over" as we say. They will choose to stay at the energetic vibration they enter when the spirit leaves the body. These are the "ghosts" of which we speak. My first encounter with one of these energies was when I was training to receive messages from kids on the other side. I was communicating with a spirit of a girl named Sarah. I felt a presence with me and asked if it was Sarah, and I heard, "No. My name is Ed." He felt heavy and I knew this was not Sarah!

Since these energies really do not understand your path, it is very important to identify where they sit energetically. Therefore, I teach my students how to determine the energetic vibration of any spirits they contact, which you will learn also in this workbook!

Clair

The Clairs are how we receive information through our senses. I have included a quiz to help you determine which is your "dominant" clair, the one that is stronger than the others. We all have access to all of the clairs, but there will be one or two which are more pronounced than the others.

Clairsentience is "clear feeling." This is feeling in your physical body. It could be a vibration, goose bumps and/or aches. It could also be that "gut feeling" you have about someone or a situation.

Clairaudience is "clear hearing." This is hearing words in your head which may or may not be in your own voice. I am fortunate that I hear other people's voices so I can determine if I am speaking with a man, woman or child. For many, it might sound like your own thoughts, which makes it challenging to distinguish if it is your own thoughts or whoever is communicating with you. Set your intention to hear them, and what you hear will be them. You may need to work on believing this really is your loved one, angel or guide. I had many doubts about my abilities, but I continued my training and connecting, and it was well worth it in the end.

Clairvoyance is "clear seeing." This can be seeing energies as waves or outlines. It can also be seeing pictures in your mind. My first clairvoyant encounter was with the father of a friend of mine. I never met him and knew nothing about him. He worked with my sight to bring very clear pictures his daughter validated immediately. After I got off the phone with her, I was ecstatic! I could finally see! It was not as I had imagined it, which is why I bring this up. I remember thinking I had to see those on the other side in order to be a true medium. This is not the case. Using any of the clairs to receive information is being a medium. Also, many mediums call themselves clairvoyants, which may or may not mean they can see spirits. Some use the terms interchangeably, which can be confusing. We will learn a little later how to identify if this is your dominant clair.

Claircognizance is "clear knowing." Those who have claircognizance as one of their clairs just receive information, as if it falls from the sky into their heads. They have no idea from where it comes. It is just there. Many men are claircognizant. They think they are just really smart to have all of these answers they just know, without realizing they are actually receiving this information from the Divine. It can be challenging to accept the information is not from you because it is so intrinsic. Many claircognizant individuals will need to work on trusting the information they receive.

Chakras

The chakra system is important to understand for your training. Chakra is the Sanskrit word for "wheel". The basic chakra system consists of seven energy centers in our bodies that each corresponds with certain physical, mental and spiritual functions. We keep our chakras as clear and open as we can during training because blocks in our energy centers can translate to blocks in receiving. A blocked chakra means the energy is not flowing through that energy center and there is an imbalance in your system. You will have an exercise later in this workbook to work on your chakras, but I wanted to address how each of them is defined. These are the definitions I use, but they are not the only definitions out there. Different philosophies look at the chakra centers from other perspectives, so use your intuition to find what is right for you.

Root Chakra

The root chakra is located at the base of the spine. The color associated with this chakra is red. Our root is about our security, our foundation, and feeling safe. If this chakra is blocked, we might have money and fear issues, and feel like we are not supported.

Sacral Chakra

The sacral chakra is located right above the root chakra. The color associated with this chakra is orange. This is our creativity center and sexuality center. A blocked sacral chakra could relate to feeling like we are not creative or feel shame around our sexuality. We might feel less than or not worthy.

Solar Plexus Chakra

Our solar plexus is located in our stomach area. The color associated with this chakra is yellow. This is our power center. A blocked solar plexus might translate to over-controlling situations or people because we feel powerless, or giving our power away. We also hide our fears in our solar plexus. When we meet someone who is not for our highest good, we feel it in our gut, or solar plexus. This chakra tells us if something is safe for us or not.

Heart Chakra

Our heart chakra is located in the center of our chests. The color associated with this chakra is green. Our heart chakra is where we give love and receive love. It is also where we hold our wounds. A blocked heart chakra might translate to not feeling loved, or not feeling like you are loveable. It might also be where we withhold love because of our wounding.

Throat Chakra

Our throat chakra is located in our throats, of course. The color associated with this chakra is sky blue. Our throat chakra is where we speak our truth and ask for what we need. A blocked throat chakra could evidence itself through sore throats and other throat related dysfunction or disease. If you were told you should be seen and not heard, or ever chastised for standing up for yourself as a child, your throat chakra might need some clearing.

Third Eye or Brow Chakra

Our third eye or brow chakra is located in the center of our foreheads. The color associated with this chakra is indigo. Our third eyes are our windows to the other worlds. It is where we connect with our psychic-ness and where we "see" energies. A blocked third eye chakra might make it hard to connect to the other side or believe you have the ability to do so. Many very powerful souls have blocks in their third eye chakras because of persecution of their abilities in past lives. They feel it is unsafe to use their sight in this lifetime and block their ability to see into the other side.

Crown Chakra

The crown chakra is located at the top of the head. The color associated with this chakra is violet. This is our connection to the Divine. It is by opening our crown chakra that we can receive clearly. A blocked crown chakra might evidence itself in the inability to receive guidance and messages from our helpers. Some imagine this chakra opening like the lotus flower blossoms, and this chakra is often depicted as such. If you get frequent headaches, you might need to open your crown a bit more.

Angel

I ask the angels for daily assistance, whether it is to help me raise my vibration, surround me with protection, boost the energy in my body, or assist in my healing from illness. They find me great parking spots, also!

The word "angel" comes from "angelos" which means "messenger" in Ancient Greek. Angels are our infinite helpers. They assist us in living on Earth. They protect, guide, and intervene when necessary to keep us out of harm's way. Unlike guides, angels bring us unconditional love, whereas spirit guides have personalities and often carry the traits they had when they were in bodies. Angels are a purer form of energy. They have very powerful energy, can be in many places at once, and have an infinite energy source.

Angels have been recognized by many cultures, pre-dating the Christians. The Ancient Greeks had "gods" with angel-like qualities, such as Hermes who was considered a messenger of

God, and in Rome, where he was called Mercury. The Vikings also had a messenger God called Hermod.

Guardian angels are angels who stay with us and guide us gently throughout our lives. They will manifest in human form if they must to save us from a lesson to which we did not agree.

Archangels

The Archangels are special helpers. Again, they have infinite energy and can be in multiple locations at the same time. They each have a specialty, although you do not need to know whose specialty is whose. You can call on them at any time for any reason. You are never alone. You always have your Archangels and their unconditional love.

The Archangels with whom I work on a daily basis are:

Michael – the protector. I call Michael the Cosmic Bouncer because he will remove any energy around you at any time. He is with me twenty-four hours a day, seven days a week. I call on him whenever I need that extra boost knowing I am protected and safe. If you look at pictures depicting Michael, he usually has a sword. He does not need a sword, however. He is powerful on his own.

On more than one occasion I can recall waking up in the middle of the night and sensing an energy right above me. Of course, I immediately call to Michael and ask him to remove it so I can go back to sleep. I will usually ask him in the morning who was visiting me, and he will reply "a helper" or "a healer." I usually apologize for my haste, but ask my helpers to make sure they do not wake me up! It is nice knowing, though, that Michael will remove them no matter what.

Michael also helps me when my computer needs some healing. He assists with all things electronic, so be sure to call on him before kicking your computer to the curb!

Raphael – the healer. Raphael helped with the construction of the body and its systems. He understands the physical form more than anyone. He also rules the heart, both physically and emotionally. I call on Raphael whenever I need emotional or physical healing. He and I work together to figure out what needs to happen for true healing to take place. He is an amazing energy, and when you call him in, you feel your heart warm like never before.

Gabriel – the messenger. It is said that Gabriel was the angel who came to tell Mother Mary she was pregnant. There are many references to Gabriel in various religious books. For me, he is someone to talk to. He helps me with my communication with others, and he just listens when I want to gripe. He can help me see others' perspectives when I do not understand what they are trying to say, and works with me very closely when Mercury is in retrograde (an astrological event that often results in misunderstandings with others and problems with contracts). Call on Gabriel when you need help communicating or writing. He can come as a male or female, depending on what you need.

Ariel – the soft one. Ariel is a very strong yet feminine energy. After my encounter with Ed in the beginning of my training, Ariel protected me from those types of energies. At the time, I needed a feminine energy to help me come into my own power and strength. Whenever I called to her, she was there. She gave me the assurance and confidence to continue my work. I knew she would be there, no matter what. She embodies courage and strength, but with a feminine feel.

Guide
Spirit guides come in many forms including human and animal. The term "Spirit Guide" generally refer to those not in bodies who watch, teach, heal, and help us on our way. They are high vibration energies and see our paths in ways we cannot see from our perspectives.

Spirit guides can go by many names. They are not attached to any names we call them. The names are really for us and not them.

Each guide generally comes to you for a specific purpose—creative abilities, healing issues, spiritual development, so it is possible for guides to come and go during your life depending on where you are on your path and what you need at the time.

Your guides do use signs to communicate with you. They might use birds, music, dreams, and toys, just to name a few, to get your attention. Enhancing your communication with your loved ones also gives you access to your guides. Use the exercises in this course to assist you with this connection.

Animal Guide or Messenger

An animal spirit guide may appear to give you a quick message for the immediate issue at hand, or this guide might follow you on your path to help you discover who you are. Having an encounter with an animal guide will have a different feel to it. Maybe you have never noticed the hawks in the sky, and suddenly you look up and see one. Or a rabbit runs in front of you as you walk or drive down the road. That is an animal guide with a message. Great resources for animal spirit guides are books by Steven Farmer or *Animal Speaks* by Ted Andrews.

A few animal spirit guides and their meanings are:

> Bear – Strength
> Coyote – Trickster
> Deer – Gentleness
> Dog – Loyalty
> Eagle – Connection to Creator
> Lion – Leadership
> Mountain Goat – Surefootedness
> Rabbit – Fear and Timidity
> Raven – Connection to Spirit
> Turtle – Slow and steady

Animal guides can have multiple meanings and messages so be sure to go with what resonates with you or the situation.

Common Questions

The following are common questions I am asked at my live events. I wanted to include them in this workbook to help with your training.

Can my loved one hear me when I talk to him/her?

Absolutely! Whenever you talk to your loved one, think of him or her, or grieve, he or she is right beside you. Remember, they see you very differently now. The past is the past.

Did he/she make it?

YES! Trust your loved one is exactly where he or she needs to be. We always have help and there is always someone close by to assist our loved ones if there is any confusion or complications at their passing.

How do I know it is my loved one sending me a sign?

If the thought of your loved one crosses your mind, it is a sign. As soon as you think of your loved one, he or she is there. Sometimes, they give you the thought of them in conjunction with something else. Watch for the subtleties!

Does my loved know I love him/her?

Of course! All your loved ones love you very much. That is the one thing we take with us: love. Love is what binds us and connects us, no matter where we are, no matter what the circumstances.

Are they finally out of pain?

Those of us who have had to watch the slow, painful passing of our loved ones are usually concerned about this. Once our loved ones cross over, all pain and suffering disappears. They have memory of it, but not the experience of it. As time goes on, they understand why they had to leave the way they did and how this affected others around them. Part of their work now is to help us come to terms with our experience of their pain and passing.

I had an argument with my child right before he/she passed. Does he/she know I am sorry?

Your child sees you with love and understanding. It does not matter what happened here. Of course, your child forgives you and wants you to let go of the guilt you feel. There are no exceptions to this. Forgive yourself. Your child already has.

What did my loved one see when he/she passed?

This varies from person to person. Many will see Jesus if they expect to see Jesus. Many will see other loved ones who went before them. Many will just see the light and feel the incredible peace and love all around them. This peace and love is limitless and gives a feeling of safety and security.

A dear friend of mine, Kris Pauplis, went back home in 2012. She had a long convalescence with cancer. A couple of days before she left, she was talking with someone who certainly was not in a body. When her husband asked her to whom she was talking, she replied, "the boy right here." There was no boy in body in the room. I knew it was J.T. When Kris and I had conversations about what her life would be like after she released her body, J.T. would pop in and reassure her he would walk her through it. It was so comforting to both of us. Her husband did not know about his promise, so to him, she was hallucinating.

Other people have told me similar stories about their loved ones seeing "dead" relatives prior to passing. I know one thing for certain: we are never alone when we leave.

My loved one was very mean to me. I am not sure I want to even talk to him/her.

Your loved one now sees his/her part in what happened. They are no longer in the emotion or ego of the situation. Sometimes, they might come through with this personality so you recognize them, but they will immediately show you how much they love you.

An example of this occurred during one of my Connecting to the Other Side events. A man came through telling me he was the father of one of the audience members. He was looking for his son. I described him and a picture he showed me. It was of a boy with a German shepherd. I could see the picture so clearly, but no one was claiming the man. Finally, a woman raised her hand and said, "I think you are talking about me." She clearly was not the man's son. I looked at her puzzled. She told me her father wanted boys. He had all girls, no boys. Her name was Jackie. She told me he was not the most pleasant father, and this was verified by the man who was telling me some things which were certainly not pleasant. I was having a conversation with him in my head telling him he'd better shape up or I will stop the connection. He told me, "She won't believe it's me if you don't tell her what I said." I understood what he meant. If your father was a mean man and the spirit who claimed to be him was nice, would you believe it was him? No. He had to be nasty in order for her to believe it really was him. He softened immediately and started giving me messages from the heart, transforming into the soul he truly is now.

I was so compelled by Jackie's dad I looked her up on Facebook. I had a feeling I would find the picture her dad showed me of Jackie and the dog. Sure enough, there it was. I was astounded at how clear her father was. Jackie had very short blonde hair and was dressed in overalls standing beside her dog, just like her father claimed!

I learned a lot about Spirit that night. "Things are not always as they seem! Keep an open mind and the answers will be clear," they tell me.

Where Is Heaven?

Where did my son go? I asked my mentor, my guides and anyone else I could, trying to wrap my brain around this new reality in which I found myself. I am a very detail-oriented person. By trade I was a Software Quality Assurance Engineer prior to having children. I also did my fair share of process flows during some document management consulting when I was starting a family. These are left brain functions—the logical side. So much of what I was learning about connecting had nothing to do with logic and I had to accept that. My trust and faith in what I was doing was stretched to the limit. I am an open-minded person and accept others' truths. At the same time, I am skeptical and rely on logic to be the ultimate authority.

Logic is not a word I would use for this world in which I now live. The concepts I am sharing here are what I know to be true for me. I am always learning, though, and getting more pieces of the puzzle, so this concept might morph a bit here and there. At this point, this is what I understand about where J.T. and our loved ones reside. I am keeping this general so you can get the basic concept. I invite you to put it through your own filters, use your own vernacular to understand this and explore with your loved ones to find your own version of the story.

There are different dimensions, as we call them. Different levels of energy reside at each of these levels. Here on Earth, we are in the third dimension, for the most part. Energetically, we are dense because we are in bodies and live on a dense planet. Those who die and leave their bodies go to the fourth dimension. They are still close enough to our vibration, so we can sometimes see them and interact with them, especially those of us who are very sensitive. As they release their "stuff" from their lifetime, they move to the higher dimensions—the fifth and above. It is with the fifth dimension and above where most of my communication takes place. I can and do converse with the fourth dimension, but I do not receive guidance from any energies in this dimension since they are not high enough to see our highest good.

There is not a "place" for these dimensions. My understanding is these dimensions occupy the same space. When I call to J.T., he has to come down to my vibration to communicate. He is not coming to a place; he is coming through the different levels of energy to meet me where I am.

This does not mean we are all on top of each other, though. There is plenty of room in our Universe for all of the energies to have the space they need to do whatever work that needs to be done.

Do animals go to heaven?

Many beloved family pets come during my readings. I usually see them bound in and jump on their owner. They may rub up on my legs if I do not notice them come into the room. During a Connecting party I connected with a very special dog for a blind lady. It was her guide dog who she had to put down a year prior. His message to her was she made the right decision. He was tired and wanted to go home. It does not mean he doesn't come to visit, though!

Many of my clients request to speak to their animals because they feel guilty about their pet's passing and want to be sure they did the right thing. Without fail, the animal comforts the owner by saying they did exactly what needed to be done.

Animals are very unique in that they usually hang around in our dimension for a lot longer than human spirits, so you might hear them running down the hall or feel them jump on the bed. I have had clients who tell me they even make room for their pets on the bed because the feeling is so strong. When they look for the animal, there is no one there!

What is Reincarnation?

Reincarnation is the belief that we have past, present and future lives. Too many psychics tell parents they cannot contact their children because they have reincarnated. This makes my blood pressure skyrocket and all the veins in my neck pop out. It is simply not true. Our children will always be available to talk, whether they were one week old or ninety years old. We can even converse with those souls who were born sleeping and miscarried. How is this possible? Again, everything and everyone is energy. Anyone who has incarnated even for a few weeks is energy. If we know the laws of energy, it cannot be destroyed—it only converts to something else.

I know I have had past lives and have spent many of them with my current family members. We each have had different roles and lessons we provide for each other. My mother has been my mother in many lives and we are still teaching each other the same lessons. J.T. has been my son in many lives, also. We like the closeness of the mother-son bond. Similarly, my husband has been my son and my daughter has been my sister.

I know this because of the many past life regressions I have done with Brian Weiss, M.D. and the information I can now access psychically. Learning about my past lives has healed and explained many of the experiences I have had. I do not dwell on them. I get the information and put it into my own reference. Learning about past lives should not make you feel more victimized or helpless. It should assist your healing and understanding of what you are doing now.

I have included past life regression information in the Resources section if you are interested in pursuing this.

Will I be bothering my loved one if I ask them to come connect with me?

There was a time when I was told J.T. had to leave for a while to go "learn." I was devastated. I thought it would be forever until he came back and we could talk again. At the time I still knew so little about where J.T. was. He was "gone" for two days. He came back in a short time, and I worried he came back for me and I was holding him from moving forward. He explained that there is no time where he is, so two days or ten days; it had no reference where he was. He also told me he could be in more than one place at once. I wondered how my seven year old could do such a thing! I was reminded since he was not tied to Earthly time, he wasn't really seven anymore. Yes, he would still come to me in whatever form I needed and he would age for me if that helped me, but he was now an infinite soul. It took some time for me to assimilate this very foreign concept into my very logical mind.

Over the years since J.T. left, I have been given many of these types of messages. J.T. plants the idea by saying something a certain way, and then he waits a couple of days and tells me the next piece. I think he knows my brain would implode if he gave me all the information at once! The concepts he explains to me are always mirrored in my readings or others with whom I speak, as if I needed the outside confirmation of what he told me. Of course, I need the validation. Sometimes I think my hearing has gone haywire. Hearing the same idea or information from another source is way for Spirit to say, "You see? We weren't messing with you. We really meant what we said!"

Part Two: Weekly Exercises

This section is broken into weekly exercises. Take a full week to assimilate the information for a particular week. Even if you feel you understand it completely, take the week. Do not rush this process. I had a student who took the psychic workbook I was using at the time and read it cover to cover in a month. She came in for her monthly training session believing she knew everything she needed to know about being psychic. What she did not understand is that this is an experiential process and sometimes you need time for the information, ideas and connection to solidify in your mind, body and spirit. My teaching guides have created these exercises to help you with this and they can see what you need. Trust them and you will be amazed at your success!

Week One: What Do You Believe?

This week we look at your belief system. At least twice this week, answer these questions based on how you perceive them at that time. Observe any changes to your answers during the week. Make note of these changes in your journal.

> When you were a child, what did you believe about heaven and hell?
> Did you believe what you were told or did you feel there was more to the story?
> What do you believe now about heaven and hell?
> What has helped you form this belief system? Family, friends, life events? Explain in detail as much as you can.
> How is this belief system different from the one with which you were raised?

When J.T. first left, all of my beliefs about heaven and hell left with him. I didn't know what to believe. I was raised Catholic, but felt there was always more to the story. In my first book, I

21

wrote about driving up the mountain when I was seventeen with the purpose of driving off, until a voice in my head said, "If you do this now, you will just have to come back and do this all over again." This was not my own thought. I had never contemplated reincarnation before, so I know this did not come from me. It made sense, though, and I believed it enough to turn my car around and drive back down, mumbling all the way, "Like hell I'm doing this again."

It was also at this time that I met the energy I call God. My relationship with God was not very comfortable. I didn't like the idea of someone sitting on a throne judging me as I did my best down here. When my brother died in 1981, that changed. My brother came to me in a dream to let me know he was alright. Behind him was a figure in the shadows. I knew it was God. I told God at that time, "You get me through this, and I will pay more attention to you. You have to lead the way, though, because I am really confused right now and don't think I can see where I'm going." A sequence of events followed this dream and I know it was God leading the way for me.

> What does the term "God" bring up for you?
> Are you comfortable with that word? Yes/No
> Do you have another word you use for this energy?
> With what kind of God were you raised?
> Harsh and judgmental? Loving and kind?

What I found during this process of losing my brother was a loving God, not the God I was told to fear in religion class. This made all the difference to me as I walked through my life. There were times when I still could not use the word "God." It had a negative connotation for me. I started using "The Universe" and "Source." I was talking about the same thing; I just needed to call it something other than God.

The importance of this is simple. If you believe in a harsh or judging God, you may not be willing to open yourself up to your angels, guides and loved ones for fear of damnation.

If this is the case, what do you need to have it be okay to communicate with the other side? This is a very important question, so be sure to take some time and answer it completely and honestly. What will make it okay for you to communicate with the other side?

Now that you have written that down, ask for it! Ask for whatever you wrote on the line above to come into your awareness right now. Begin by taking a deep breath and exhaling completely. Say, "I am asking for (what you wrote) to come into my awareness right now. Thank you." Observe what happens.

Did anything shift for you? Yes/No

If you do not sense any change, wait a day and see what happens. Something in your awareness will change, if you want it to and if you asked for it with sincerity. Sometimes we find it is not God who is in our way, but us. We hide behind the idea of God not approving because we are scared or don't know how to step into our power. By reading this book, you are saying to God, The Universe, Source, "I want this. I want to lead a guided life. I want to communicate with my loved ones." And the answer that will come from heaven is, "We've been waiting for you! What can we do to help?"

The next part of this exercise is:

> Where do you believe your loved ones who
> have passed are now?
> Do you believe they are far away? Yes/No/I
> don't know
> Do you believe they are right beside you?
> Yes/No/I don't know

If you feel they are far away, you may not believe they can hear you or that they will come when you ask them to. I called to J.T. so many times during the day; I was sure he was getting sick of me and would eventually not show up. I was wrong. Whenever I called to him, he answered. Whenever I asked him a question, he answered. Whenever I thought of him, he was there beside me. I learned that he is with me all of the time, sometimes closer to my dimension, sometimes farther away. There were times when there was a delay in the answer, as if he had to come through the levels to reach me. Then other times, it was immediate.

I have learned when you think of your loved one, they are beside you. When you call to your loved one, they are with you. Believing this helped me understand I could ask a question at anytime and receive the answer, no matter what. Can you accept this as your truth? Can you believe your loved one is beside you right this very minute as you read this (maybe even peering over your shoulder critiquing my writing)? I hope you can, because that will get you one step closer to clear connection.

Making It Real

Call to your loved one, angel or guide throughout this week.

> Do you sense them with you when you call them? Yes/No/Maybe
> Observe and journal each time you think of your loved one, angel or guide this week.
> Is there a pattern or sequence of events that precedes or follows the thought of your loved one?
> Over this week, what has changed, if anything, about your belief system?
> Why has this changed?

Week Two: Creating Your Space

This week we look at the space around us—our homes, our offices, where we spend our time. It is about observing and creating.

> Where do you spend most of your day?
> Is this where you want to spend your time?
> Do you have a special space you can call your own?
> If you do, how much time do you spend there?

If not, get ready! You will need to create it this week! Being a mother, wife, animal lover and student, a place of solitude and peace did not exist in my house. Once I hid in my bathroom to talk to Zane's mom to give her messages from her boy on the other side. Zane was that first spirit who woke me up in the middle of the night to get me to contact his mom. When I did finally reach his mom, the bathroom was the only place that was private and had a lock! I realized after that I needed to create a space that was mine and mine alone. I am also blessed to have an office outside of the home to which I can escape when I need to have even more concentration, such as writing this workbook.

The space in which you live, work and play is critical to your connecting success. If you do not have a special place to meditate or work through this book, you may miss some of the details and get distracted. I know for many of you this may seem impossible. Here are some suggestions.

> Take a room separator or folding screen and claim your space in an existing room.
> Clear out a section of the basement and make your space there.
> Turn a spare bedroom into your meditation room.
> Create a sign for the door on a current room that says, "Work in Progress" and let the entire household know if the sign is up, they

will need to find another way to solve their issue.

This is something you need to do for *you*! You need a quiet place to regroup at least once a day, especially when you are learning to communicate with the other side. This is not a "would be nice to have." This is a "must have." Put yourself first and create your space now!

Making It Real

For the rest of the week, work on creating your space. Buy some pretty candles, flowers, a comfortable chair, a bookcase for your books, maybe a desk for your automatic writing (which will come later)—whatever you desire in this space to make it a place of comfort, peace, solitude, and refuge. You will spend time in this space every day. Make sure it is what you want.

> Where is your space?
> What did you put in your space?
> When you sit in your space, what do you feel?

Week Three: Clearing and Protecting Your Space

A common hesitation when beginning this work is the fear of inviting something dark into your life. I understand this and learned very early in my training that I am in charge and what I say goes. Period. It took time before I felt powerful enough to uphold the boundaries I set. In the meantime, I was introduced to the angels. It is the angels' job to help us in whatever way they can. I realized when I did my connecting work at the outset, I was afraid; I did not open up completely. Once I acknowledged this, I received instruction on how to call on the angels to clear my space, raise its vibration and protect me 24/7.

It is important to feel safe when you connect. Fear holds us from moving. Learning how to clear and protect yourself and your environment will help you get to the next level and be successful with your connecting work.

There are many ways to do this clearing. For me, the easiest and most effective is to call on the angels to help me. They will clear my energy, the energy in my house and clear any stale or unwanted energy, wherever it may originate. I found asking Archangel Michael for assistance extremely effective. Archangel Michael is so close to God's energy and is the highest on the vibrational scale. I call him the Cosmic Bouncer since he will remove any energies I ask him to remove for my highest good, and will not allow anything in that does not belong. Trust him; he gets the job done!

When asking for his help, remember it is all about intentions. Be sure your intentions are clear, no matter what you are intending! You do need to believe he can help you in order for him to do this.

For this week, do the following.

Clearing Your Space

> Take a few deep breaths.
> Center yourself and open up to the Divine.
> Repeat this prayer:
> "Dear Archangel Michael, please vacuum out
> my house, each and every room, removing

any energies that are not for our highest and purest good, or our Divine purpose. Please use the high setting and replace any energy with your light and love. Thank you so much."

What happened to the energy in the room when you did this exercise?
Exit the house and come back in. Does anything feel different?

Clearing the Energy From Your Body

Before you begin your connecting work, it is a good idea to remove any energies you might have picked up during your day. Archangel Michael can also help with this.

Take a few deep breaths.
Center yourself and open up to the Divine.
Repeat this prayer:

"Dear Archangel Michael, please vacuum any energies out of my body, my aura, my energy fields and centers that are not for my highest and purest good or for my Divine purpose. Please use the (high/medium/low) setting and replace any energies with your light and love. Thank you so much."

The settings "high" "medium" and "low" are how slowly or quickly Archangel Michael removes the energies. Play with it and see what fits for you.

What were you sensing when Michael was clearing your energy?
How did you feel after he was done?
Can you think of other applications for this prayer?

You can repeat this exercise anytime you feel you might have picked up some lower energy somewhere, and for your house whenever you feel it needs a boost.

Protecting and Sealing Your Space

I wanted to be sure I was only dealing with the highest vibration when I was learning to connect. By doing the exercise below, I was certain only high vibration was allowed in my house. To this day, my house is sealed and protected, and only high vibration is allowed inside.

> Take a few deep breaths.
> Center yourself and open up to the Divine.
> Repeat this prayer:
> "Dear Archangel Michael, please seal this house, doors, windows, ceiling, floor, wall to wall so only high vibration is allowed inside. All other vibrations must stay outside this house from this moment forward. Thank you so much!"
>
> What do you notice about the house or space now?
> Exit and come back in. Do you notice any difference in the energy or how it feels?

Asking for Personal Protection

I learned early in my training that I was a powerful medium. The light off my head that the spirits could see was very bright. I am also a feeler, so I could feel them approaching me all the time. Being a student, I could not always identify what kind of energy it was, but once I asked Archangel Michael to be my protector, I knew whoever it was, they could not hurt me. Michael is still with me all the time. I know it is because of him that I feel safe anywhere I go.

I encourage you to ask Michael to be your protector also. Here is how to do this:

Take a few deep breaths.
Center yourself and open up to the Divine.
Repeat this prayer:
"Dear Archangel Michael, please be my
protector from this moment forward.
Surround me with your love and light and
allow only high vibrational energies near me.
Thank you so much!"

That's it! If you ever feel any fear around anything, call to Archangel Michael, and he will be there. I can attest to his protecting wings around me. Walking to my car late at night, or entering a house I know is haunted, I call to him. He is always there!

A note about this last part, you might still feel lower vibrational energies around you since we do still live in the third dimension. Archangel Michael protects you from their attachment (unless you allow this), but he cannot keep them out of your surroundings. They cannot hurt you, though, unless you let them.

Do you sense Michael with you? Yes/No
How are you sensing this?
Do you feel protected and safe? Yes/No
How do you know this?
Do you believe Michael is protecting you now
and from this moment forward? Yes/No
If your answer is "no", say the prayers again
and see if you have any change in how you
feel.

Making it Real

The other task for this week is to create a physical representation of what your protection looks like. This could be drawing a picture of Michael watching over you. It could be buying an angel figurine and putting it in your house or car. You can also use clay or even Play-doh to make your own angel. Whatever works for you and whatever will remind you that you are protected will do the trick.

Remember, the more you raise your vibration, the higher vibrations will surround you and the lower vibrations will seem farther away. So keep those vibrations high. We will have exercises in later weeks to help with this.

Week Four: Learning to Meditate

The simplest way to quiet the critical thinker is to meditate. When I was told meditation was the key to communication with my son, I almost quit right there. I took a meditation class in my thirties in Berkeley, California—I tried and tried, but I couldn't clear my mind. I would think of the grocery list or whether I fed the dog—mundane things which occupy our thoughts. When it was clear to me that I needed to meditate to hear J.T., I decided to give it another try. I used a guided meditation. In a guided meditation, I concentrate on a soothing voice and my left brain is listening to the words and instructions while the right brain is working on connecting. By using a guided meditation, I was able to satisfy my left brain by giving it something to do. It had to listen to the words of whoever was guiding me. I became a very successful meditator. Now I no longer require a guided meditation to meditate. I can do it through my breath, music and energy..

What is your definition of "meditation"?
Do you meditate? Yes/No/Sometimes
Have you tried to meditate in the past? Yes/No
What gets in the way of you meditating?

Meditation is not a technique but a way of life. Meditation means "a cessation of the thought process." It describes a state of consciousness, when the mind is free of scattered thoughts and patterns. "Watching your breath" is meditation. Listening to the birds is meditation. As long as these activities are free from any other distractions to the mind, it is effective meditation.

The word meditation is derived from two Latin words: meditari (to think, to dwell upon, to exercise the mind) and mederi (to heal). Its Sanskrit derivation 'medha' means wisdom.

With a regular meditation practice, your connection to Source, Spirit, Creator, God—that Infinite Energy—is enhanced and becomes clearer. Meditation is the key to connection!

Meditation also raises your vibration, which is the frequency at which your soul vibrates. The higher the frequency of your energy, the easier it is to hear, see, feel and know the Divine.

The best time to meditate is in the morning, although anytime is good. Meditating in the morning sets the tone for the day. You begin your day at a higher vibration, which can make a big difference in how the day progresses.

If you cannot find time to meditate in the morning, do it whenever you can. It only takes fifteen minutes to raise your vibration through meditation!

Each and Every Day

It is essential you make time every day to develop your meditative practice and habits. This can be challenging at first, but once you start the routine, you will notice a difference in your outlook on life and your ability to connect. It can take some time to do this, and you must make it a priority.

There are many ways to meditate. You do not have to use a guided meditation. You can do a walking meditation where you take a walk and just observe what is around you. See how crisp the leaves on the trees are. Smell the air. Let your senses take everything in. This is meditation! Another form of meditation is gardening, or painting pottery or anything creative. I have a student who meditates as she crochets. The hand movement as she crochets is enough to keep her left brain busy as her right brain takes her on that journey to meet her guides, angels and loved ones.

Do what works for you, make sure you do it. As I have said before, it quiets the critical thinker and allows the right brain to take you on that journey of connecting with your Infinite Support System.

This week, research meditation. Answer these questions during this week:

> What stops you from meditating?
> What music do you prefer when sitting quietly?
> Do you like to walk? Yes/No/Sometimes
> Do you like to ride your bike?
> Yes/No/Sometimes
> Do you like to garden? Yes/No/Sometimes

Do you like to paint or draw?
Yes/No/Sometimes

Making It Real

Explore the internet, libraries and bookstores for meditation CDs. Download samples and give them a try. Do you prefer soft music? Do you prefer being guided? Is it easier to just use your breath? The point is to find something that works for you. Brian Weiss has some wonderful meditation CDs. Look for at least two or three meditations that call to you. Meditating is a practice which needs to be done on a daily basis. Using more than one will keep you engaged and not bored with the same thing every day. Once you find something you would like to try, include it in your daily schedule. Meditate every day for fifteen minutes. Try meditating in the morning, evening, afternoon. There is no right or wrong way so make sure it feels right to you.

At the end of the week, answer these questions:

> What time of day do you feel you were most successful at meditating?
> What kinds of meditation worked best for you?
> Were you able to meditate every day? Yes/No
> If not, why do you think this is?
> Going forward, what kind of meditation do think will work best for you? Guided? Walking? Breathing?

Week Five: Quieting Your Critical Thinker

The next step to connecting is to begin the process of training your mind, or as I call it, the critical thinker, to accept we can communicate with those we cannot see. Our minds are powerful. They keep us safe from harm and they create logical steps for us to follow—"two plus two equals four, and the quickest way from point A to point B is a straight line." Connecting to the other side, however, does not follow this logical pattern. "If it is not logical, it should not be attempted. You are crazy to think you could do this."

Thinking will not get us connected. Instead, we use our creative side, the right brain. The left brain, our mind and ego, might tell you something to sabotage your progress because it "thinks" it knows what is best. In my connecting training, one of the hardest things I had to do was to quiet my critical thinker.

This week, explore the ways your critical thinker runs the show. Keep a journal of each time your critical thinker pops in and tells you this is crazy to do this, or you need to be logical about it, or this just isn't going to work, etc. Write the day, time and message you got from your critical thinker.

> We are going to take each of these messages from our critical thinker and change it up a little bit! Read each of the lines you wrote above aloud and say, "Thank you, Critical Thinker, for protecting me. I can take it from here. What is true about this is _____"

An example would be:

"Day: 5/13/13 4:30p It's my own thoughts I'm hearing, not anything from my angels." You say, "Thank you, Critical Thinker, for protecting me. I can take it from here. What is true about this is I know it was not my voice I was hearing. I know it was my angel."

The point is to change the way that thought is programmed in your brain by stating your own truth about what you are receiving.

> What was the overall message your critical
> thinker is trying to tell you about this process?

Making It Real

Each time your critical thinker gives you a message about not
being able to do this work, repeat the following (in your own
words): "I know I can connect and I know I am a clear
receiver."

Again, what you are doing here is replacing whatever
thought your critical thinker gave to you with an intention. Use
your own words in your intention. Be sure to put something to
the effect of "I know I can do this" in your intention.

> What intention did you use when your critical
> thinker gave you a critical thought?
> Other ways to quiet that critical thinker
> include:
> A walk in nature.
> Meditation.
> A quiet drive in the country.
> Listening to calming music.
> Doing anything creative.

Play around this week and see what works for you.

> What did you find was the most effective way
> to quiet your critical thinker?

Week Six: Grounding

Grounding is a process of planting your feet firmly on the ground and calling in all your energy to be in your body. For humans, it is a "direct electrical connection to the earth." What grounding does for us is it pulls us back into our bodies. We spend a lot of time in our heads, thinking about what we are doing next, what we will eat for dinner, how we will pay the bills. By connecting with the earth, we pull our awareness away from the mind and into the center of our bodies. Our heart center and power center (solar plexus) are where all the connecting to spirit begins. If there are pieces of our energy floating around but not really present, it is difficult to become aware or recognize the signs and communication around you.

The easiest way to ground is to sink your feet into the earth, literally. Since this may not be possible year round, below are other methods of grounding which have worked for me.

First, take a deep cleansing breath. Breathing deeply clears out our inner cobwebs. Imagine there are roots going from the bottom of your feet all the way to the center of the earth and then imagine these roots attaching themselves there. If you are feeling particularly flighty a certain day and having a hard time feeling rooted, take those roots and imagine you are wrapping them around the core of the earth a few times. If you still are not feeling grounded, imagine a cord, called a grounding cord, coming from the base of your spine stretching all the down to the center of the earth and attaching to the center of the earth. If you can't seem to make it to the core of the earth, get as deep as you can. The point is to feel sturdy, like a tree.

There are other ways to ground you can incorporate in your day. Go for a walk in nature. This can be a form of meditation. Gardening is another wonderful way to ground. In the winter, it might be a challenge, but there are always ways to play in the dirt, even in the winter.

> Practice grounding from the bottom of your
> feet, extending roots from your soles and
> plant them deeply in the earth, preferably to
> the center of the earth.

What do you notice about your body when
you dig your roots into the earth?
Can you sense any difference in your body or
your awareness? Yes/No
If so, what is different?

Remove your roots from the earth. You can
cut them off or imagine they disintegrate.
Can you sense any difference now that you do
not have your grounding?
Reattach your roots now. What do you notice
is different now?

We are going to use a grounding cord in this
exercise. Imagine there is a cord at the base of
your spine. It can be any material you would
like, as thick as you like and whatever color
you like. It is attached firmly at the base of
your spine (your tailbone) and it extends all
the way into the earth to the center of the
earth. Imagine it wraps around the center at
the core.
How does this feel?
Do you feel more grounded or less grounded
than with the roots grounding?
What color is your cord?
Why do you think you chose this color?
What does this color mean to you?

Detach your grounding cord from the base of
your spine and let it fall into the earth.
What do you sense?
Reattach your cord. What do you notice that
is different?
Which method of grounding do you prefer?
Why do you prefer one over the other?

This week, practice grounding at least seven times each day.
When I learned how to ground and connect, I put sticky notes

around the house, in my car, everywhere, reminding me to ground. Sitting at red lights, I would check my grounding. I had the tendency to not be present in my body. I had to practice my grounding. Don't get discouraged if you feel you are not getting that connection to the earth. Just keep practicing.

Making It Real

Get those crayons out! The other task for this week is to draw what you see for your grounding. If you prefer roots from your feet, draw this on a piece of paper. If you prefer the grounding cord from the base of your spine, draw that. Make sure you represent how far into the Earth your roots and cord go. This is very important. Put this drawing somewhere you can see it throughout the day so you will have another reminder to ground.

> Can you say you are grounded now? Yes/No
> If the answer is no, what might be helpful to
> do to get grounded?

Week Seven: Setting Intention

Setting intention is telling the Universe, guides, angels and your loved ones what we expect from this experience called LIFE. I use the following prayer of intention and suggest you use something similar each time you begin any psychic or connecting exercises:

> "My prayer of intention is that I clearly hear, feel, see and know all that I need to know today. My intention is also that I boost my abilities to receive from my angels, guides and loved ones. I am a clear receiver and the information flows easily. Only positive, loving high vibration energies are allowed to communicate with me right now, and I invite you in now, all those who wish to assist me today. I am so grateful to be able to do this. Thank you for your help."

This prayer has all of the points we want to include whenever we are connecting:

> What we expect from ourselves and our helpers
> Only high vibration can connect with us
> We know we can receive clearly
> We are grateful for the connection.

If there is someone in particular with whom you wish to connect, invite them in. It is a great idea to include gratitude in your prayer. God, Source, The Universe, the One, whatever you call that Divine energy, responds very well to gratitude!

It is important to phrase your intention from the positive perspective. For example, if you were to include a phrase "So and so cannot come in," this would be from the negative perspective (cannot). The Universe does not always hear the "not" or "no" in your prayers, so instead phrase it to ask for what you *do* want. "Only so and so can come in to speak with me right now" is an appropriate intention.

It is your turn to set your intentional prayer.

> What do you want from this experience?
> What is your prayer of intention? Write it in
> your journal.

Making It Real

This week, say your prayer of intention each morning when you wake up and whenever you are doing any connecting exercises. Print it out and tape it to your mirror in the bathroom or the dash of your car. The more you set your intention, the easier it is for the Universe to bring it to you!

Week Eight: Chakras

Let's work on our chakra system and get the energy flowing so we are clearer receivers. The chakras are energy centers located in our bodies and each corresponds to a physical, mental and spiritual function. By working with these and clearing any energetic blocks, the energy can flow better and we become better receptors. There is an exercise each day this week as we concentrate on each chakra.

Day 1 – The Root Chakra

Today we work on our root issues. Answer the following questions to determine how the energy is flowing in this chakra:

> Do you feel safe in your life? Yes/No
> Do you feel abundance in your life? Yes/No
> Do you feel supported in your life? Yes/No

If you answered "no" to any of these, you might have some blocks in your root chakra. Regardless, follow the exercise below to keep this chakra cleared.

Today, your affirmation is "I am safe and supported in all areas of my life." Throughout the day today, repeat this phrase. Even if you are not feeling this is 100% true for you at this time, say it anyway.

Each time you say the affirmation, close your eyes and ask Archangel Michael to bring a big red ball of energy to help you clear this chakra. Envision him handing you this red ball and then put the red ball into your root chakra while saying, "My root chakra is now cleansed and cleared." This clearing exercise is all about intention, so if you say it is cleansed and cleared, it is.

Day 2 – The Sacral Chakra

Today we work on our creativity and sexuality center. Answer the following questions to determine how the energy is flowing in this chakra:

Do you feel creative? Yes/No
Do you feel comfortable in your body?
Yes/No
Are you ashamed of your sexuality or being
the sex you are? Yes/No
Has anyone ever told you they wished you
were the opposite sex of who you are?
Yes/No
Have you ever had disease or dysfunction in
your reproductive organs (endometriosis,
infection)? Yes/No

If you answered no to either of the first two questions, or yes
to any of the last three questions, there could be blocks in this
chakra. This is very common in our society because of our
shame around our sexuality and our emphasis on left brain,
logical thinking over right brain, creative thinking.

We are going to take that first step to change that
perception. We are going to *create* something today! Get some
clay, dough or another type of moldable material and take
fifteen minutes (at least) to create something that represents
you. This could be something you love to do, or something
you would love to have in your life, or even an actual
representation of who you are. Some examples of what I might
create: a microphone, because I love to speak; a smiley face; a
clock, because I want more time during my day; a book
because I love to read. Don't skimp on this exercise. We open
our creative centers so we become clear receivers. This is as
critical as opening our crowns.

What did you create today?

Day 3 – The Solar Plexus Chakra

Today we work on our power center. Answer the following
questions to determine how the energy is flowing in this
chakra:

Have you been giving your power away to
others? Yes/No/Maybe
Are you trying to control events, situations
and people over which you have no control?
Yes/No/Maybe
Do you have frequent digestive issues?
Yes/No/Sometimes
Have you been called a control freak?
Yes/No
Did you feel powerless as a child?
Yes/No/Sometimes

Most of us felt powerless to some degree as a child. After all, what child is allowed to have control and power over their own decisions until we are deemed "old enough" or "mature enough"? The difference is if your parent, guardian or authority figure used the control over you to dictate how you behaved, what you did or with whom you spent your time. If this was the case, your parent, guardian or authority figure misused their authority.

Do you continue to let others control who
you are?

Now is the time to reclaim your power! This does not mean turning the tables or seeking revenge. It is going into your third chakra, cleaning it out and reclaiming what is yours. Remember, we are all children of God and we are all powerful. We do not need to control others. We stand in our own power and in who we need to be here to get the job done.

Hold your hand over your solar plexus as much as you can today and say the affirmation, "I am a powerful soul. I call all my power back to me."

How does that feel to say those words?
Write down what it means to reclaim your
power.

Day 4 – The Heart Chakra

Today, we work on healing our hearts. For many of us, this is a tall order. We have been wounded from the time of our birth, and sometimes even before that. Healing these heart wounds is a one-day-at-a-time process. Today, let's focus on one wound.

> Hold your hand over your heart and ask your heart what is the most important wound to heal today? Write your answer in your journal Trust what you receive from your heart. Are you surprised by this answer or did you expect it? Yes/No
> If you are surprised, why?

Beginning to mend this wound is simple—ask for your Divine helpers to work with you throughout the day to heal:

> "Dear Divine Helpers, please help me to heal this wound in my heart today."
> Then let it go. At the end of the day, do a check-in. Place your hand over your heart and ask, "How is the healing of this wound now?" Write your answer in your journal.

If what you receive is not complete, ask your helpers to continue working on you as you sleep. If it is complete, thank your helpers for working on it with you today.

Whenever you are ready to work on healing more wounds, follow the exercise above. Some scars take longer than others, but your intention to heal is paramount. Keep healing and keep clearing out the old junk. Your heart thanks you for your hard work!

Day 5 – The Throat Chakra

Today, we focus on our throats. This chakra is where we speak our truth and we speak from love.

When you were a child, were you told to be
quiet or to shut up often? Yes/No
Did you feel you could not tell others what
you really felt because of their reaction?
Yes/No
Do you get afflictions of the throat often –
sore throats, strep throat, etc.? Yes/No

If you answered yes to these questions, your throat chakra
probably needs clearing. Today we are going to sing!

Put your hand on your throat and sing the following song:

I'm a little teapot, short and stout
Here is my handle, here is my spout
When I get all steamed up, hear me shout
Just tip me over and pour me out!

I'm a clever teapot, yes it's true
Here's an example of what I can do
I can change my handle to my spout Just tip
me over and pour me out.

How does your throat feel now? What did you
feel when you were singing?

It is fine if you did not feel a shift in energy in your throat.
Some people sense the shift immediately after this and some
don't. Regardless, know you have opened your throat just a
little bit more than before the song.

The other thing we will do today is speak our truth.
Whenever you encounter a situation where ordinarily you
would just keep quiet, not ruffle any feathers, speak up! Always
ask for grace and compassion when expressing yourself so
what you say can be heard by the other party. This does not
mean you get to unload on the person who has held you from
speaking. Be kind and know they might not understand what
you are doing, but do stand up for what you want. Special
note: If you ever feel physically threatened, please get

appropriate assistance before speaking up, i.e., a witness or proper authority. Don't ever put yourself in danger.

We will do something nurturing for our throats now. A warm compress, hot or iced herbal tea, wearing a necklace that makes you feel like a queen or king. Treat your throat like royalty!

What did you do for your throat today?

The last thing you will do for your throat today is write a letter to someone telling them how you really feel, or how their actions affected you, or why you were hurt, or anything else you need to get off your chest. You do not have to send your letter. Just the act of writing it will help release stuck energy in your throat chakra.

Day 6 – The Third Eye Chakra

Today, we work on our third eye or brow chakra. It is located in the center of our foreheads. Yours might be tingling right now as you read this. That's Spirit's way of saying, "You have sight!"

We use our third eye as the window to the other worlds. It is our clairvoyance, and our connection. We will work on opening this chakra complete and fully. Today is about removing any blocks in our third eye chakras so we can connect and "see" clearly. We often have blocks in this area if we were psychic kids who had to shut down our abilities because either it was too scary or just not acceptable in our homes. By shutting down our sight, we severe our connection to our angels, guides and loved ones.

I had a hard time opening my third eye because I was fearful of what I was going to see. I heard about the crazy things people would see. I learned, though, that opening my third eye was the ticket to connecting to where my son was. I kept my intentions clear on why I was opening my third eye and the Universe responded accordingly. It helped me tremendously to connect to the higher dimensions.

Your first exercise today is to release the fear of seeing. Fill in the blanks for the following intention:

> "My past fear of opening my third eye is
> _____ but I know now the Universe will
> show me only love and light and high
> vibration, so I am ready now to open my third
> eye chakra completely and fully."

> Repeat this intention through the day and
> know you are safe and protected!

If you cannot identify any fears around opening your third eye, then do the following exercise today:

> Place your hand over your third eye and send
> energy (through intention) to your third eye
> via the palm of your hand. This is done simply
> by saying, "I now send high vibration energy
> from my hand to my third eye, cleansing and
> clearing this chakra and opening my third eye
> completely and fully to receive."

You will sense a shift in energy with your third eye chakra when the energy exchange is complete. Then, remove your hand, close your eyes and imagine that your third eye is open.

Observe throughout the day any insights you receive via your third eye or any changes in your connection and journal them in detail.

Day 7 – Crown Chakra

Having a blocked Crown Chakra has a similar effect as a blocked Third Eye. Information has a harder time getting to us. Learning to open our Crowns will allow flow of energy from the higher dimensions and give us a better connection. Again, we might have closed our crowns as children because too much information was coming in and created confusion with our world view. I have had many students complain about headaches and not understanding why they can't receive from

Spirit. When I check their crowns, I usually find they are almost closed with just a slight opening. This creates a situation where too much information is trying to come through a small opening, thus creating pressure in the form of a headache. I ask my clients to put their hand (either one) on their crown and with their intention, open their crown so the information can get in and out. This is what we will begin with today.

> Place either of your hands on the top of your head with your palm touching your head. Say, "With my intention, I open my crown to receive from the Divine." Remove your hand. What do you sense is happening now with your crown?
> Do you sense any lightness? Yes/No/Maybe
> Do you sense the opening? Yes/No/Maybe
> Check in and ask for your helpers to give you some input through your crown by saying, "Divine Helpers, please help me check how open my crown is now by giving me some information. Thank you!"
> Did you sense any new information come in? Yes/No/Maybe

It is fine if you didn't sense anything. Some people are very sensitive and others are not. It has nothing to do with your psychic abilities, only that it gives you feedback and validation. It has everything to do with how you receive information.

Think about the exercise above as you answer the following questions:

> Was I comfortable opening my crown today? Yes/No
> If not, why not?
> Did I have any fear around opening my crown? Yes/No/Somewhat
> If yes, what was the fear?

49

If you cannot identify the fear, ask your helpers to assist by giving you information about this today. This might come in the form of signs, words, messages from others, or some other way. Be observant and see what happens.

> What did you receive from your helpers to help you identify anything about your crown chakra?
> Do you sense you are more connected by opening your crown? Yes/No
> From what you have learned so far, what can you do to feel more connected?

Week Nine: Breath

Breathing is very important in connecting with our angels, guides and loved ones. It opens the energy centers, raises our vibration, and helps us to receive. There is a difference between "normal" breath and true breathing.

True breathing is also called "belly breathing." For most of us, our breath stops right at our heart center. Stop for a minute and pay attention to your breath. Your lungs are actually below your heart center. When you belly breathe, your lungs should fill with air, making your "belly" rise. Your exhale should be full, letting all the air out.

This week, we will learn to breathe to connect.

Each day this week before you get out of bed, take a moment to breathe deeply. Close your eyes and breathe into your stomach. Hold for a moment, then release. Do this for at least five breaths. The more you stop and breathe, the easier it will be to connect. Here are some common steps you can use this week to learn your belly breathing.

> Getting ready:
> Blow your nose if it's stuffy
> Sit or lie down in a comfortable position
> Close your eyes
>
> Belly breathing:
> Place your hand on your belly
> Inhale through your nose into your belly so your belly rises like a balloon
> Slowly breathe out through your nose, using your stomach muscles to push your belly back in until all the air is pushed out
> Try to make your exhalation last at least as long as your inhalation
> Keep breathing in and out slowly for a few minutes

If you begin to yawn, use it to push out more air. Yawning is a very natural way to release energy.

Breathing deeply is important because it helps open our senses. By breathing deeply and deliberately, we awaken our senses to receive information we might not receive otherwise.

Mindful breathing is the same as above, but we are going to use a four count in and a four count out.

> Take a deep full breath. As you breathe in, count to four slowly
> Exhale fully as you count to four again.
> Continue this for at least 10 full breaths

As you are breathing on the four counts, keep focused on a single image in your mind. A big oak tree would be good if you cannot think of anything else. If other thoughts come in, push them aside and bring the oak tree or other image back to your awareness.

After you complete this, concentrate on your body. It should feel relaxed and energized.

> Does your body feel relaxed and energized after this breathing exercise?
> What did you learn about your breathing when you did this exercise?
> Was this a difficult exercise for you to do? If so, why?

Making It Real
Breathing is a great way to relieve stress. Should you find yourself in a difficult situation, take a moment to breathe deeply and exhale completely. Release all that energy from your body. I find I can see the situation much clearer after breathing into my body.

> What do you notice when you breathe deeply?

Put post-its around your house, in your car, at the office which simply read, "Breathe deeply." Remember to take a few deep breaths several times each day. It helps connection to your helpers.

Week Ten: Forgiveness

We have such high expectations of ourselves and others here on this planet. When people in our lives fall short of our expectations, we can feel bitter and cheated. We are fallible and we do things we regret or that we wish other people did not do to us. I can think of many things my family and friends did in my life that I resented for many years. It was not until I began this journey after J.T. left that I found my own lack of forgiveness of others and myself was holding me from receiving clearly.

Forgiving others and ourselves for being human seems like something we should do without hesitation, but our culture does not support this idea. We are taught we need to be as perfect as we can. When we or others fall short, we hold judgment, anger and guilt, just to name a few. To be clear receivers, we must forgive ourselves and others. This is a process, and you are not expected to do this flawlessly, so work on this as much as you can this week. Be forgiving of yourself if you are not ready to consider these issues. Give it time and space. Keep in mind that as you forgive yourself and others, your connection to Spirit will open significantly.

Making It Real

In your journal, make a list of the people in your life you have not forgiven. On the left side write "Name of person" and on the right side write "Deed to be forgiven." Be completely honest and write down everyone and everything you can think of. Remember this is your list and no one will see it.

Do not judge any of this—whether or not they deserve to be forgiven, whether or not you feel guilty about not forgiving them. Just write it down.

For each of these people and situations, ask your helpers to help you forgive them. Take one situation each day this week and during meditation, imagine that person is there with you and asking for your forgiveness. Ask yourself:

> What do you need from them to forgive them?

Consider, "Do I really need this or can I
forgive them without this?"
What believe system, if any, is keeping you
from forgiving them?
Do you still believe this?
What needs to change within you to forgive
this person, regardless of what they can or
cannot give to you in return?

Work this week at being the observer of your forgiveness. This
exercise is about you looking at these situations and people
from a different perspective, freeing you and them from the
past, and freeing that energy from holding you.

In your journal, record your observations from this exercise.

Did it surprise you when you found it difficult
to forgive someone?
Did it surprise you to be able to forgive so
easily?
What else did you observe about you this
week with regards to forgiveness?

Week Eleven: Forgiving Yourself

Last week we worked on forgiving others. This week, we will work on forgiving ourselves. Many of us are more willing to let others off the hook than ourselves. We cannot value who we truly are if we are not willing to forgive ourselves. We may not feel worthy of happiness and we feel guilty about the smallest things we see as mistakes or imperfections in our core. This creates a barrier between us and our helpers on the other side. If we do not feel deserving, we will not open up to receive communication.

Your angels, guides and loved ones have a unique perspective. They hold no grudges; they have no anger or disappointment. They only have love and want the best for you. No matter how your loved ones passed, if you feel any guilt around how they lived or left, release it. They have already forgiven everything that happened in their life. It's very important that you forgive what happened also.

Guilt and unforgiveness are very low vibration emotions. They stifle your ability to move forward with whatever you need to do in this life. Our loved ones are there to help us and absolutely do not want to see us suffering because of guilt or non-forgiveness. It has an effect on whether you receive messages from your loved ones, not because they are mad at us, but because your negative emotions are blocking the messages.

No matter how uncomfortable this next exercise is, please give it a try. Forgiving yourself will definitely help your connection with your loved ones, angels and guides.

Making It Real

Just as we looked at situations with others where forgiveness was in order, we will consider situations where we need to forgive ourselves. This might mean going back to childhood when you were mean to someone in school. Or it might be in a current relationship where you judged someone for their actions. Give yourself the same opportunities you gave to the people last week. Truly work at forgiving yourself for anything you might have done.

Being a mother who had to bury a child, I held an abundance of unforgiveness for not saving him. After all, I was with him at 4am, left him for two hours, and he was gone when I came back. I spent many a meditation working on forgiving myself. I realize, of course, he needed to leave and no matter what I did to stop it, he would have left anyway. It took a long time to release myself from this burden. I encourage you to do whatever you need to do for self forgiveness. This is critical to the success of your connection to Spirit.

> We begin with a list. On the left side of a page, write "Deed to be forgiven" and on the right side of the page, write "Reason(s) I have not forgiven myself." Complete this page as frankly as you can.

Now we take each of these deeds and examine them individually. As with last week, we will use meditation as a means to forgive. Before you enter a meditative state, ask your helpers to assist in releasing you from this deed and to help you forgive yourself. During meditation, ask for the energy of that person or situation to come. See it as a very high vibration energy—not the energy that is incarnated here on the planet, but that of an angel or angelic representative. The angels love us no matter what. They truly give us unconditional love. Take whatever it is that you need self-forgiveness and hand it to this angelic energy. Tell this energy you are sorry for having taken so long to forgive yourself and you now accept you are here on this planet to learn. You are not expected to be perfect. If we were supposed to be perfect, we would have stayed in Spirit form! Ask the angelic energy if there is anything else you need to do to release this, and then follow the instructions. Journal your meditative experience as soon as you come back to your awakened state.

Take one of the deeds each day and use this meditation exercise to forgive yourself. If you feel up to it, you can do two a day. By the end of the week, hopefully you will have cleared most of the items on your list.

What did you observe this week about forgiving yourself?

Week Twelve: Asking for Help

This week we look at asking for help from our helpers and others to propel us on our journey.

Answer these questions:

> Are you the type of person who feels you
> need to do everything yourself to ensure the
> job is done right?
> Do you have a hard time asking others for
> help when you need it?
> Do you remember the last time you asked for
> help?

My answers to the questions above would have been *Yes, Yes* and *No*. I had no idea how to ask for help without looking or feeling vulnerable. There were many situations in my life where I felt controlled and I had no intention to go back to that place in my life again. It was hard to ask for help from my helpers because of my past. First, I did not feel deserving of their help. Secondly, I did not have the confidence they would actually show up. I learned through the passing of my son that I really needed help. It was the one time in my life I could not do it alone.

If you are like me, please take time with this exercise. Your helpers want to show you how much they support you and how much you deserve to have their assistance. Keep an open mind this week, and be observant to your surroundings. Your helpers will be aiding you with everything from finding parking spaces to feeling safe.

If you accept help easily, this will be a fun week for you to explore your helpers. Ask and you will receive!

> This week, ask your helpers to find you an
> excellent parking space. Be sure to give them
> enough time to clear one for you – in other
> words, don't wait until you are in the parking
> lot! Ask when you leave the house. The words
> for this could be, "Helpers, please find me a

parking spot right in front of _____ store.
Thank you so much for your help."

Remember to always thank the helpers. Then don't think about it again until you get to the store and see what happens. Do this at least five times during the week. Once, you might think is a fluke. Five times is not a fluke.

> What happened when you asked for the
> parking spaces?
> If you received the spots, do you believe it
> was your helpers who cleared the spot for
> you?
> If not, what do you think created the parking
> spot for you?

If you are not receiving great parking spots, look at your belief system again.

> Do you believe you are worthy of their help?
> Do you believe they want to help you?
> What do you sense is keeping you from
> receiving their help?

Making It Real

Keep asking for those parking spots, and when you are ready, ask them for other things as well. Ask for assistance to find something for which you are looking. Ask to clear the path for you to get to work on time, to bend time a little so you aren't late for your appointments.

One caveat to this is they will not bring you anything that is not for your highest good. Lottery numbers are probably not going to fall in your lap, but rest assured, if you need to find your keys, they will help bring them to you!

Week Thirteen: Setting Boundaries

Common questions I hear are "Will I be able to turn it off?" or "Will they overtake me?" Television media creates this illusion that those with "the gift" cannot shut it off and will be at the mercy of those on the other side, with no regard to your desires. In the beginning, I did not know it was possible to turn it off, and I wanted to connect and get messages from kids on the other side to their bereaved parents. I felt it was my duty to be "on" all the time. My children were five and three at the time, and I remember on more than one occasion (especially when I was changing my son's diaper) a spirit would "buzz" me to chat. I obviously had to finish one task (changing the diaper) before I began another, but because of my open door policy, the spirits were rather insistent I stop what I was doing and take their message.

One night while I was in bed asleep, I felt the vibration of a spirit trying to get my attention. This was usually the way J.T. would begin our communications, but it was the middle of the night! I asked J.T. why he would need to wake me up – he, of all people, should know I needed my sleep! I told him I loved him but he needed to go away.

The following night, the same thing happened. It was about midnight and I was awakened by this vibration in my body. By this time, I was getting a bit irritated with my son. "What, J.T.? What do you need that is so important it cannot wait until morning?" J.T. said, "It's not me." I panicked a little. After all, I was only in training for a month at this point. This was such a new life for me; I was clueless how to handle the situation. My connection skills had not come in fully yet, and I was leery since I had no idea who this was. It felt like a boy, and he was insistent I work at getting his message, regardless of the time of night. I told him he must go away and return when I got some help to decipher things.

The following day, I called my mentor and explained what happened. We both tuned in and I was able to receive the message. This was my first encounter with a spirit I didn't know. I felt accomplished and so excited! Spirits were coming to me and I was receiving clearly. *I really am a medium.* I realized that I needed to set my boundaries. This very persistent soul did not care if it was the middle of the night. He wanted to reach his mother!

I set my "working hours" as a part of these boundaries. When spirits came to me to get a message to their loved one, I said, "I am working today from this time to this time. During that time, I will ask you to come in and we can get the message. Any time other than that, I am not open to receive." It worked, and I was able to sleep uninterrupted.

If you want to connect, you need to make the time, but it does not have to be on *their* time. Those of us still in bodies have the priority. We are the bosses here. You can tell them to go away until you are "working" and they must abide by your wishes. I learned with some spirits I needed to be firmer. They were as pushy in the afterlife as they were here.

Lisa Williams, a renowned medium, has a hat she wears and the spirits know when she is wearing the hat, they need to wait to connect with her. I used this visual when I was setting my own boundaries. I would put my hand on top of my head and say, "My hat is on. I am not receiving messages right now." I would always qualify this, of course, that my angels, guides and J.T had permission to come whenever they needed to contact me. After all, they are my support system.

This week, we work on setting boundaries for connection. Remember, you are the boss! Think about limits you want to set, what you are willing to do and what you are not willing to do. Answer the following questions:

> What are your "working hours" (when you want to receive communications with the other side)?
> With whom do you wish to communicate during that time? Angels, guides, loved ones, others' loved ones? Be specific.
> Do you have any fear about opening up to this communication? If so, what is that fear?
> What do you need to do to alleviate about connecting with your angels, guides and loved ones now that you have set your boundaries?

Making It Real

Every morning when you wake up this week, reaffirm your boundary.

"I __(name)_____, will be working
from _____ to _____
today/tomorrow/day. During that time I
accept communication from _____.
I am the boss and these are my boundaries!"

Week Fourteen: Observation

You observe the world around you this week. Observation enhances your abilities. It allows you to be more in tuned, thus receive more messages from your angels, guides and loved ones. These exercises will require time outdoors, so if the weather is questionable, feel free to wait until the weather is suitable for this task.

Find a quiet place, preferably without distraction from cars and people. Use all of your senses to answer these questions:

What do you see?
What color are the things around you?
Ask your helpers to enhance the color of these things for you. What changes did you notice? What color is the sky? Are there clouds in the sky? Which way are the clouds moving? What pictures do you see in the clouds?
Are there any birds flying? Can you identify what kinds of birds?
Are the birds giving you any messages by flying closely to you or squawking at you? If they are, what is the message? Ask them what they are trying to tell you and write it down.

What do you hear? Close your eyes and tune in to your hearing.
What do you notice that you did not notice with your eyes open?
Now open your eyes. Do you still hear what you heard when your eyes were closed? Are there any noises that are different?

What do you feel? Close your eyes and feel your surroundings.
What do you notice around you?
Did you notice this when your eyes were open?

What are you feeling in your body?
Open your eyes. What changed now that your
eyes are open?
Did any of the sensations change?

What do you smell now?
Close your eyes and tune into the smells
around you.
Is there anything you smell that you did not
smell with your eyes open?
Can you identify what you smell?
Open your eyes. Did the smell change?

The point of these activities is to tune into all of your senses. Our sense of sight sometimes fills in the blanks. With our eyes closed, we can heighten our other senses and get more information about the environment around us.

Making It Real

Practice this at least three times this week in three different locations. Write down all of your observations.

Week Fifteen: Identifying Your Dominant Clair

How Do You Receive Information?

Answer the following questions to see how you receive information through your senses. Whichever section has the most "yes" answers determines your "primary clair." It is guaranteed you have the ability to connect through all of the clairs, but for training purposes, we work first with the dominant or primary clair to communicate successfully with the other side.

Are you a "seer" (clairvoyant)?
When you first encounter someone new, do you first notice how they look? Yes   No
Can you see pictures in your mind when you close your eyes? Yes   No
When someone is telling you a story, do you see it in your mind? Yes   No
Do you see colors around people? Yes   No
Do you see colors when you close your eyes?
Yes   No

Do you "hear" (clairaudience)?
Have you heard voices in your head you knew were not yours? Yes   No
When you ask a question, do you hear the answer in your head? Yes   No
Do your ears ring? Yes   No

Are you a "feeler" (clairsentience)?
When you enter a room, do you feel the room before you see anyone? Yes   No
When you talk to someone who feels down, do you start to feel down, while they start feeling better? Yes   No
Do you feel tightness in your body when someone else has an ailment in their body?
Yes   No

Do others dictate your mood by the way they feel? Yes No

Do you just "know" what you know (claircognizance)?
Have you ever just known something without ever learning it or hearing it? Yes No
Have you ever had someone ask you a question and without even thinking about it, you knew the answer, and you knew it was the true answer? Yes No
Do answers or solutions drop into your head as if they have been there all along? Yes No

The clair for which you answered the most "yes's" is your dominant clair. This is the clair that receives information the easiest. It does not mean you will never have the other clairs, because we all have them. As I stated above, for training our clairs, we work with your dominant clair first, and strengthen it for connection. Once you receive clearly with your dominant clair, you can use the exercises in this book to enhance your other clairs.

When I began my training, I felt envious of those who could see spirits. I could hear them and feel them, but to be a good medium, I thought I had to see them, too. This turned out to be a myth. I let go of the idea of not "seeing" them and concentrated on my hearing. Shortly thereafter, I began seeing pictures in my mind and Spirit started showing me movies in my head relating to the person to whom I was giving the message. Sometimes they would show me something random, like a bouquet of flowers. I asked them, "What does this mean? Tell me what you are trying to say." That was an "ah-ha" moment. Tell me because I can hear! I didn't have to see at all!

Making It Real
Ask your guides to help enhance your dominant clair. Be observant of what they give you as validation. Keep a journal of what you see, hear, feel and know from Spirit this week. Be diligent in keeping tracking of this information. Often, the clair

we think we will be strengthening is different than the one we expect.

> What did you see this week? Were you shown
> different pictures in your mind?
> Did you see colors when you closed your eyes
> or when you were meditating?
> Were you shown something unusual this
> week?

> What did you hear this week? Did you hear
> someone else's voice or idea in your head?
> What did the voice say to you?
> Did your ears ring this week?
> Were you aware of sounds you did not hear
> the previous week?

> What did you feel this week? Did you feel
> someone else's emotions in your body?
> Did you feel any vibrations in your body or
> around particular people?
> What did you feel during meditation?
> Did you feel uneasy in any situation this
> week?

> What came to you through your knowing this
> week? Did you have a knowing about
> something of you did not know before?
> Did your guides give you a knowing about a
> situation in your life this week?
> Did you give someone advice this week and
> knew it was exactly what they needed?

Look at your answers above and thank your guides for bringing your dominant clair to your awareness.

Week Sixteen: Strengthening Your Clairs

Now that we know how we receive information, let's practice receiving.

We always begin with the prayer of intention from Week Seven. After your prayer, begin the exercise to enhance your dominant clair.

Note: If during any of these exercises you sense information that has a negative tone, these are not your angels and guides. It could be your mind and the old tapes playing from your childhood or programming, or it could be something else. Regardless, stop the exercise and set your intention again. Ask for your angels to come closer and then continue the exercise. If it still feels negative, ask your angels to help you remove the negative energy, wherever it is coming from, and then resume. Usually it is just our minds playing with us.

Clairvoyance

Clairvoyance is sometimes misconstrued as being able to see spirits. Yes, this is part of it, but more than this, it is seeing images or visions in your mind.

Being clairvoyant might mean you see people's energy, see auras, see mists in the context that they are souls or spirits. You are also clairvoyant if you see through your mind's eye. This would mean seeing pictures of those on the other side. You might see it in your mind like a movie.

Keep a journal and include all the times you are given "pictures", or when you see energy.

You can also journal any symbols Spirit uses to convey a message, like "roses" might mean love or an anniversary, balloons might mean birthday, etc. These symbols will be used over and over by Spirit, so it is a great idea to keep track of them.

> If seeing is your dominant clair, close your eyes right now and ask for your angels and guides to come help you with this exercise. Note: This exercise will have its best results right after meditation.

What do you see? Do you see an image or
colors?

You can practice your clairvoyance by asking your Infinite
Support System to open this clair even more and give you
pictures and colors when you are meditating.

Your second exercise for this week is to sit and observe a tree.
Trees have auras. See if you can "see" the aura of the tree.

Sit comfortably near a tree.
Center yourself and ask your helpers to
heighten your sense of sight.
Look at the tree – try to not blink if you can.
How far out does the aura extend from the
tree? Does it have color or is it white?

If you are not seeing any aura, ask the tree to help you see its
energy. If you ask nicely, it will be more than happy to help.

Practice with other objects in nature. Every living thing has
energy around it.

What did you *see* this week? Write out every
detail you recall.

Clairaudience

Your dominant clair is clairaudience if you hear answers from
Spirit. This might sound like your own voice, but the inflection
and/or words might not be something you would ordinarily
say.

An example of this is when I was on the phone with the
medium who said, "You are clairaudient. You can hear them."
I said, "No, I can't." Suddenly in my head another voice said,
"Yes, you can." I knew these were the high guides with whom
she was speaking. They felt very powerful and I knew my
success hinged on learning how to listen to them. So I said, "I
guess I can!"

I also had Archangel Ariel by my side 24/7 to help me
with my fear of the lower energies. Whenever I would call to

her, "Are you there?" a soft loving voice would respond, "Yes, I am here."

It can happen just like that. You hear "Mommy" and turn around to find no one is there. That could be your child on the other side calling to you. Maybe you hear your name in your head, in your voice or someone else's. This could be a loved one or guide.

You can tell it is Spirit and not just your mind by the way in which the questions are answered. Spirit will not say anything negative or make you feel like you did something wrong. Spirit is loving and understanding. Sometimes, as with Archangel Michael, the voice is powerful and commanding, but again, they will never ask you to do anything that would put you in harm's way or say anything to make you feel badly about something you did.

How to tell whether the "voices" in your head are yours or not:

One trick I learned was to ask my questions aloud. That way the answer didn't sound like it was coming from me. For whatever reason, doing this differentiated my voice from whoever was answering. I also suggest sticking to questions that can be answered "yes" or "no" in the beginning. This makes it very simple. If the voice sounds critical in any way, remember, it is not coming from Spirit. That would happen to me occasionally where my critical thinker got in the way and thought "it" knew the answer. Because I doubted myself so much in the beginning, I asked the same question different ways numerous times. You will drive yourself crazy if you do this. Trust. This is about trust.

To enhance your clairaudience:

First ask for this clair to be enhanced. A very simple prayer is "I ask that my ability to hear Spirit, God, the Universe (whatever you call this realm) be opened. Please allow my hearing to be clear and concise. Thank you so much for this opportunity to hear you." Another way to put it is, "I know my hearing of Spirit is getting clearer and more concise." Then believe it. Believe you can hear. We all have that connection to the other side.

Another way to enhance clairaudience is to do automatic writing. With this technique, you are writing what you are hearing, not what you are thinking.

If clairaudience is your dominant clair, practice automatic writing this week:

> Begin with a meditation
>
> State your prayer of intention: "My intention for this automatic writing session is that I hear clearly and that only the person/energy I ask to talk with me is allowed to come. I know I am protected during this session and I thank my helpers for this assistance." For this exercise, we ask for the guide who is assisting with your hearing to come.
>
> Sit at your computer with an open word processing document or at your desk with a pen and paper.
>
> Ask "Who is here with me?" and then type the answer. Keep your eyes closed and just type or write what you hear in your head. Do not censor or edit.
>
> Keep asking questions and writing the answers.
>
> When you feel the session is complete, thank your helper, open your eyes and read your document. Save these documents and date them. You will be amazed at the information you receive.

Clairsentience

Clairsentience is when you can feel your loved one is around, but don't have any "proof" of it. You just feel it. This could be through sensing they are near, or a sensation in your body. During those first months after J.T. left, I would feel a tingling sensation on my left hip when I cried. I thought I was going crazy, until someone told me it was J.T. giving me a hug. I thought about it and the tingling was at the right height where his arms would reach around me.

If you feel before you see, know or hear, then clairsentience is your dominant clair. Spirits use my clairsentient abilities to get my attention. They send a vibration on my body, like a tickling feeling. I also can feel how a person passed, or maybe if the person smoked or had chronic pain, because that pain occurs in my body even though it is not mine. It is also the feeling that you are being watched, but turn around and no one is there.

Enhancing your Clairsentient abilities:

The first exercise is to determine what you feel in your body as "yes" and "no" answers. You are creating the way in which your guides, angels and loved ones will communicate with you.

> Get comfortable, ground and clear yourself of any thoughts or energies that are not for your highest good.
>
> Say prayer of intention such as, "I ask that my feelings be heightened for this exercise and that the answers I receive are clear and concise. Help me to raise my vibration to meet those of my angels and my guides. Only high vibration loving energies are allowed to answer me. Thank you for your assistance."
>
> Ask yourself a question that you know the answer is yes, i.e., my name is _____. Feel into that answer as it sets in your body. Does it feel light or have a certain texture to it?

> Do you feel "yes" somewhere in your body?
> Then ask yourself a question that you know
> the answer is no, i.e., I am a male in this
> lifetime. What does that feel like?
> Is it heavier, does it tingle somewhere?
> Mark the differences down in your journal
> and keep practicing until you are sure how
> "yes" and "no" feel in your body.

Next, we identify male energy vs. female energy.

There is a distinct difference between male energy and female energy. If you are a feeler, it is important for you to identify whose energy is in front of you.

Follow the same instructions with the grounding and prayer of intention. We are also asking for protection since we call in angelic helpers. The protection prayer is "I ask that I am fully protected and that only high vibration, loving energies are allowed to come near me. I also call on Archangel Michael to oversee this exercise."

> Get cozy and ask your "yes" and "no"
> questions to make sure you are tuned in. Once
> you feel like you can tell the difference
> between the "yes" and "no", ask for
> Archangel Ariel to stand in front of you. Her
> energy is incredibly light, yet powerful.
>
> How does Archangel Ariel feel to you? Do
> you feel her energy somewhere in your body
> in particular?
>
> Thank Archangel Ariel and now ask for
> Archangel Michael to come stand in front of
> you. What do you notice that is different? Do
> you feel his energy somewhere in your body
> in particular?

He should also feel very high vibration, but there is a different frequency with his energy. See if you can compare the two in your mind so you can better determine male vs. female energy.

Thank Archangel Michael and close the
session by saying, "I now close this session.
Thank you to all who assisted me today."

It is all about becoming clearer and raising your vibration so
you can trust what you are getting. Practice this every day.

A special note to feelers: You are magnets for energy. You
absorb other people's energy and definitely need to set
intention around how much of that energy comes into your
space. Before your feet hit the floor in the morning set your
intention about what you are going to "feel" for that day. My
intention is this: "My energy is mine and their energy is theirs."
You must keep the boundary between you and others. You do
not need to take away people's pain by absorbing it into your
body. It is their pain and they need to deal with it. Many of you
feelers are already healers. I encourage you to find a healing
modality that resonates for you and learn it. This allows you to
heal others without taking it on yourself. It is not healthy to
absorb other people's energy.

Claircognizance

Claircognizance is "clear knowing." This is when you have a
thought you know is true, but you have no idea.

This clair can make you think you are going crazy. Many
people are claircognizant and just pass it off as being "smart."
What is happening, really, is that Spirit gives them information
as thoughts. It is very elusive because you can't really put your
finger on why you know what you know. You will learn how to
discern from where the information is coming through
practice.

Some examples of claircognizance are:
> Knowing driving directions without ever
> having been at the location
> Knowing the answer to a question you would
> have no way of knowing
> Knowing exactly what to tell a person without
> really knowing the person
> Knowing someone is lying to you

Knowing events will occur before they occur

To tell the difference between your thoughts and "inspired" thoughts, ask yourself:

Is this something I would know?
Is there any ego attachment to it?
Does this seem like it is from me or my
spiritual guidance?

The differences can be subtle, but with practice, you will be able to tell the difference. Another way to enhance your knowing is to meditate and ask your angels to come close and communicate very clearly. Then ask a question to which you would not know the answer. You might be surprised at what comes into your head.

Making It Real
Throughout this week, your helpers will give you random messages. It is your job to be aware and open for these messages and to write them down as soon as you get them. It could be something as simple as showing you a red ball, or saying the word "red". Do not worry about figuring out what the message means. Just write it down. It will become clearer as you practice.

Week Seventeen: Who's Talking?

We all have what is called an "energetic signature." This is the frequency at which your energy vibrates. One of the exercises for new psychic medium students is to identify these vibrations.

How to Identify High or Low

I use a number line system from 0 to 10 to identify the level of vibration of the energy with which I am communicating. If an energy feels heavy or has a lower number, he or she might not have the big picture and can only give information from an earthly perspective as opposed to the higher viewpoint. They might not be aware of this at the time and usually they just want to help. Nonetheless, you need to connect with higher energies, especially during this training. This will ensure accurate information is exchanged. "0" refers to an energy that has not crossed over and feels very dense. You might get a feeling in the pit of your stomach, or just feel heaviness in your body. An energy at the "5" range will be lighter but still have a human quality to it. A "10" energy is Archangel Michael who is very light and vibrates at a very fast rate. Those at the higher end of the scale are your high guides. They know your contracts and what you are supposed to accomplish here, and will do what they can to assist you on Earth.

The following exercises will help you identify the kind of energy that is coming to you. You need to have confidence and peace of mind in what you receive. Discerning where an energy falls on the scale will give you that assurance that you know the energy with whom you are communicating has your highest interests. This week, we work on identifying the vibrational level of energies.

Use your dominant clair for this exercise and practice this every day this week.

The energy number system scale is from zero to ten:

0 – 3: Energies who have not crossed into the light

4 – 6: Our loved ones on the other side

7 – 10: Our high guides and helpers who have unconditional love for us and understand our path

To practice this, say your prayer of intention and protection, and then ask Archangel Michael to come to you. Using your dominant clair, determine where he sits on the number line. If you are a seer, you might see the number in your mind. If you are a feeler, you will feel his vibration. If you hear, he will tell you in your mind. If you are a knower, you will know the answer.

What "number" is Michael?

Next, ask for a high guide or angel to come. This energy should be somewhere between seven and ten.

What number is this angel or high guide?

Next, ask for a loved one to come. Your loved one should be somewhere between four and six. If they just left their body, it might be close to a three.

What number is your loved one?

I do not suggest you ask a lower vibration to come in at this stage of your training. You should only communicate with those energies that vibrate at a five or higher.

Making It Real
Identifying with whom you are communicating will make all the difference in your connections. You will know exactly what kind of energy is with you, allowing you to open up your senses and trust the information you receive. Practice using the number system as often as you can this week. Be sure to record your findings in your journal. You will be surprised at how successful you feel when you know the Spirit with whom you are connecting is high vibration.

Week Eighteen: Raising Your Vibration

As we have discussed, the vibration is the frequency at which everything in the Universe hums. In the beginning of this workbook I said we were all energy. Each of us runs at a certain vibrational rate. Being in bodies here on the planet, our energy is much denser than our loved ones who do not have bodies anymore. The best way to connect with them is to get as close to their vibration as possible. Things you can do to raise your vibration to meet those on the other side are meditation, Reiki, setting positive intentions and prayer, smiling, laughing, walking in nature, petting a dog or a cat. Your goal is to get as high as you can because the higher you get, the clearer you will receive. It is important to note that having a high vibration does not mean you have to be out of your body. I spent most of my life outside of my body until I went into psychic training. As counterintuitive as it sounds, you also need to be well grounded to be a good receiver. You need to stay in your body, but raise the vibration of your body, not just your spirit, to be a good receiver.

Making It Real
Have fun raising your vibration! Try different activities to get your vibration as high as you can. Note what works for you and what does not. Walking in nature might work for your neighbor, but gardening works for you. Try the following activities this week and note how you felt after doing them. If you felt lighter, happier and more connected after the exercise, add this activity to your daily routine.

> Walking in nature
> Listening to music
> Gardening
> Randomly complimenting people
> Smiling
> Laughing
> Meditating
> Writing
> Painting
> Coloring

Sipping Tea
Watching the clouds
Petting a cat (only if you are not allergic.)
Petting a dog
Watching children play
Sitting quietly and doing nothing
Reading a good book
Standing in the rain/snow
Playing in sand or dirt
Singing
Dancing
Yoga
Exercising
Gathering with friends
Paying it forward
Add your own activity here you found raised
your vibration

Week Nineteen: Journal

It is difficult for some of us to believe the hunches, the signs, and the knowing we have is really from Spirit/Source. Journaling these synchronicities is a great way to quiet the critical thinker and realize you really do get information from the Divine and loved ones.

Keep a notepad in the car, on the coffee table, and on your desk. Each time something happens that you feel might have been a sign or some other intuitive event, write down the date, time and what happened. You might be surprised at how often these things occur. Even if you aren't sure, write it down anyway.

I also encourage my students to journal all experiences they have during meditation. This is the way we integrate the left and right brains and get "everyone" on board. Writing down who you met and what happened during your meditations tells your left brain that is it a real event. Refrain from writing anything like, "I don't know if this is real or not, but..." as this will perpetuate the paradigm that you cannot connect. Treat all experiences with the other side as real encounters.

Making It Real

If you have trouble getting started with journaling, use the following prompts to help you write down your experiences:

> Date: _____ Time: _____
> Today, I _____ (fill in activity you used to practice connecting with the other side). I feel _____ (successful, not successful, confused, happy—whatever the emotion or feeling around it) about the experience. My intention for the connection was _____ (what did you want to have happen?). My experience was _____ (what actually happened). I believe the experience was real (regardless of what happened.)
>
> Date: _____ Time: _____

Today, I meditated for ___minutes. During meditation, I connected with _____ (whoever or whatever joined you during your meditation). I saw _____ (whatever visuals you received during meditation), and I felt _____ (whatever you felt during meditation). I know my experience was real (regardless of what happened.)

Date: _____ Time: _____
Today, I observed ____. It was _____ (describe what you observed completely. I was surprised by _____ (maybe how clear it was or how different it was than you thought?) I learned _____ (what did you learn from this experience?)

Week Twenty: Personal Time

We are a very busy culture, aren't we? We are programmed to believe if we are not working, we are lazy and selfish. Even with only a fraction of this programming, we are set up to fail. Why? Because you need to be self-caring in order to be the best possible you.

Every year, I take a few days away from my husband and children to recharge. I am usually attending a conference or event that will help move me to the next level of awareness, but it doesn't have to be work. I tell my children when I head to the airport, "Mommy will be a better mommy if I go on that airplane." What I am really saying is, "Man, I need a break from the responsibilities of being mom and wife and so and so's support system, etc." I need my space to recharge my batteries and give me that energy to continue what I need to do in my life. It is not being selfish. It is being realistic and required for any self-improvement.

Making It Real

This week, practice taking time just for you. Take at least 15 minutes a day, preferably more, devoted to something you enjoy doing like the activities that raise your vibration from the previous week. Fill yourself up with creativity and joy.

This might seem obvious, but how many of us do really schedule "me" time? This is essential to connecting.

We all have value, but many of us place our own value below others'. If you say to God and the Universe, "I am not as valuable as…" then we are saying we don't "deserve"" connection. Know you are more than valuable and deserve time just for you. Schedule it into your day. Tell the Universe you do value yourself!

> Write in your journal each day this week:
> What did you do to value and appreciate yourself?

Week Twenty-One: "I Am A Psychic"

By now you have done enough exercises to understand connecting to the other side is accessible to everyone. Your determination to follow through have brought you to this point in your training. This week, we will practice calling ourselves what we are: psychics.

It took a long time before I truly came out of the psychic closet. I had plenty of people in my life who would look at me like I had three heads if I said, "Oh, by the way, I talk to dead people." There came a time in my journey when I had to get comfortable with the words....psychic medium. I had to say it aloud quite a few times before I felt like I could say it to others. Of course I was concerned about being judged. I had people tell me they would pray for my soul and try to save me. I knew they were only doing what they thought they should do given the information they had at the time. They didn't realize what I could do was truly a gift from God, Source, The One, The Universe, whatever you call that power greater than yourself. Those who didn't understand had been told week after week that what I do is evil, or will bring in dark forces, or will bestow hardship on my family and anyone else within lightning range. At the time I realized I could connect with those on the other side, I was attending a Christian church. That is, until I went to pick up my children from Kids Church to find, and no joking, Leviticus 20 on the two very large screens on both sides of the room:

> Leviticus 20:27
> A man or woman who is a medium or spiritist
> among you must be put to death. You are to
> stone them; their blood will be on their own
> heads.

Of course, this is the same book that states "Your male and female slaves are to come from the nations around you; from them you may buy slaves" (Leviticus 25:44) so draw your own conclusions on what was happening at the time and how valid this is for us today.

All jokes aside, from that moment, I realized I would not be accepted, regardless from where my gifts came, and I needed to get comfortable with this and what people might say about me. I do not spend energy on correcting people who believe I am consorting with the devil. Instead, I spend energy on those who want my help and who accept the healing work I do. I set intention for my events and any other activities that only those who need my services will attend or contact me. In other words, I do not devote energy to those who feel my work is harmful. I do not feel the need to justify or prove myself to anyone. Because of this, I now rarely receive criticism about my work. When I do, I ask for the grace and love to shower them and erase their fears.

Did my revelation happen overnight? No. But it did happen. If this is a concern for you, have faith. You will eventually not be concerned about judgment or dogma and you will be able to proudly proclaim, "I am psychic!"

This week, we will practice this.

Making It Real

Each day this week, look in the mirror and say:

"I am a _____"

Fill in the blank with one of these words: Intuitive, Psychic, Medium, Spirit in a body, Angelic being, Divine Spark. The more you can look at yourself in the mirror and tell yourself this, the easier it will be to tell others when the time is right.

One more little tidbit for you if you feel you need to use this with friends, there are verses in the Bible supporting what we do. Should you feel it necessary, here's where they are: 1 Corinthians 12 and 1 Corinthians 14:1-3. Read these before you quote them to make sure you are comfortable with the verse and it conveys the message you want.

Week Twenty-Two: Gratitude

Gratitude is often reserved for the end of November when we sit around the table thanking our Creator for the turkey, stuffing and family we must tolerate, as we gorge ourselves with food and watch football. Gratitude on this journey of connecting is a daily exercise. Having gratitude for the little things raises your vibration. The higher your vibration, the closer you are to your helpers.

The year J.T. left, my teacher told us to keep a gratitude journal for a week. I thought to myself, "Oh yeah, I'm grateful my son is dead. Right. Why should I be grateful about anything? I got a bag of doggie doo here—a life without my son." I was an obedient student, however, and kept my journal. Every time I wrote something down for which I had gratitude, I felt a lift in my energy. Some days were harder than others, but each day I managed to write something. At the end of the week, I felt quite accomplished with my assignment. It taught me a lot about having gratitude and how it can help raise my vibration. Every morning, I wake up and immediately thank the heavens for the day. It is a great way to start anew.

Making It Real
Let's create a gratitude journal. Every day write down at least one thing for which you are grateful.

> Write in your journal: What are you grateful for this week?
>
> Monday: "I am grateful for _____"
> What would your life be like without this?
>
> Tuesday: "I am grateful for _____"
> What would your life be like without this?
>
> Wednesday: "I am grateful for _____"
> What would your life be like without this?
>
>
> Thursday: "I am grateful for _____"

What would your life be like without this?

Friday: "I am grateful for _____"
What would your life be like without this?

Saturday: "I am grateful for _____"
What would your life be like without this?

Sunday: "I am grateful for _____"
What would your life be like without this?

Week Twenty-Three: Lightening the Load

We live on the planet with other folks, and we are put into situations where our energy bumps into others all the time. Waiting in line at the grocery store. On the elevator heading to a meeting. Sitting in a crowded movie theater. Given we are sensitive individuals (you would not be reading this workbook if you weren't) we pick up others' energy all the time without knowing it. Carrying the junk around that is not ours weighs us down and makes it harder for our loved ones to "reach down" to us.

Lesson one for empaths (those who feel others' pain and emotions): Protect, protect, protect.

Others will gladly give you their "stuff." It is not yours to take. It is imperative that you protect yourself from others' pain and emotions because it will drain your energy. We are each responsible for our own energy, including those who are trying to give you their stuff or siphon your energy dry. The only energy you should have is your own. This does not mean you can't help others. What it means is that you will be clear and have boundaries so you can help much more than if you enmesh with other people.

Making It Real

This week, we practice returning others' energy and keeping our systems clear.

Before you leave the house, every time, state this intention: "I take only my energy with me. Only my energy is allowed to be in my aura, body and spirit. All other energies return to Mother Earth or to the spirit to whom it belongs. I am fully protected from others' energy." You can envision a golden light filling your body and your aura also. Gold is the light of protection.

Returning Others' Stuff:

> If you feel you have picked up another
> person's energy during the day, ground and
> send it down your grounding.

Say "I release all the energy in my body, spirit
and aura which are not mine or not for my
highest and purest good. These energies are
sent down my grounding and recycled by
Mother Earth. She uses this energy to create
many beautiful things."

Play with this for the week. Keep a journal and record when
you feel tired. Ask yourself, "Is this my energy, or is it
someone else's?" If it is someone else's, dump it! Also test how
it feels to be in a crowded room with your "bubble" on, and
then without it.

What's different between the two?
Can you tell when you do not have it on?
Do others notice you have a bubble, and/or
treat you differently?
Do you respond differently to those around
you when you have your bubble and when
you don't?

Week Twenty-Four: Expanding Your Bubble

Part of defining ourselves is how we relate to others. Many of us are givers and we give of ourselves until there is nothing left for us. This week, we will play with our bubble and observe how others respond.

> As with last week, repeat this intention before leaving the house, "I take only my energy with me. Only my energy is allowed to be in my aura, body and spirit. All other energies return to Mother Earth or to the spirit to whom it belongs. I am fully protected from others' energy."

We expand on this exercise now by observing where our bubble is in relation to our bodies.

> Is your bubble very close to your body?
> Does your bubble extend out away from your body?

Making It Real

With your intention, expand your bubble farther out from your body, setting your bubble bigger than it currently is. This can be as simple as saying to yourself, "My bubble now extends out another foot from my body" or imagine your bubble getting bigger and filling with more gold light.

> What changes when you make your bubble bigger?
> How does it feel to you?
> Do you feel more protected?
> Do you feel less vulnerable?

> Now, exaggerate your bubble. Make it HUGE!
> How does that feel to you?
> How do others respond to you when you make your bubble huge?

Do others even notice?

The point of this exercise is to be aware of how you are setting your space. You want to be sure you set your space to have plenty of room to breathe, but not so much that others feel cramped and vulnerable. Find the right "size" for you and make sure you set your bubble to this size each day before you leave the house. Check your bubble during the day, and reinforce it if necessary. Remember, only your energy is allowed in your space. Others need to take care of their own energy.

Conclusion: The Next Step

You have learned incredible tools to put in your Connecting to the Other Side toolbox. It is time to put it all together and create a true connection for your daily life.

We begin by practicing what we know already. We know we are psychic and we know we can communicate with those on the other side. We know we can see, hear, feel and know them. We have learned how to calm the noises, hone our clairs and work with our angels and guides to get as clear connection.

If you are a seer, practice seeing the world around you. Each day, ask your angels and guides to show you different things throughout the day. Start with asking to see auras around people or maybe what color their energy is for that day. You can also ask to see pictures in your mind about what you need to concentrate on for the day, or maybe what to expect in a meeting. Also practice seeing names in your mind. Have your angels and guides tell you a person's name by showing it to you like you are looking at a piece of paper. Begin with names you know and then move to names you do not recognize. During your meditation, ask to be shown other ways you can improve your sight.

If you are a feeler, practice your feeling sense by tuning into those around you. Instead of just going into your local coffee shop for a latte, sit for a moment and tune into the energy in the building. What do you sense? Can you tell the emotions of the person who sat in your chair right before you? Remember to dump any energies that are not yours prior to leaving.

If you are a hearer, practice your automatic writing every day. It is best to do immediately following meditation. You can also ask your guides to talk with you throughout your day. Keep your journal handy and write down everything you hear.

If you are a knower, you can also practice automatic writing (Week Sixteen). Instead of recording what you hear, write every thought in your head. Ask questions and write the answer that pops into your head. The more you do this, the more you will trust your knowing.

The most important thing to remember is to keep the momentum of your training moving forward. You have already invested six months in this process and you have worked very hard to be at this point in time. Becoming clearer takes dedication. You must continue to exercise your psychic muscles. It is a process, and just as you must take the time and energy to go to the gym and exercise your body's muscles, the same is true for your ability to connect to the other side. The good news is that you can do it. You already do it. Every day you receive information, and over the last six months you have cleared, forgiven, grounded, released and worked to get that connection. Keep up the amazing work and you will reap the rewards. I have included some websites which may help you in the resources section and some recommended reading. You and only you can keep the connection alive and well, just like your loved ones sitting beside you as you read this. Yes, that really is them and yes, they really are OK.

Memorial Section for Our Angels

This section is dedicated to all of those children who left before us. We know you have so much to teach us! Thank you for being our kids!

Aaron Earnest Roy Cann ♥ 5/19/97 ~ 5/20/97
Aaron Edward Lawrence ♥ 5/29/90 ~ 7/20/10
Aaron Marsh ♥ 8/31/85 ~ 11/9/10
Aaron Robert Simon ♥ 7/5/85 ~ 1/3/07
Abigail Georgina Cann ♥ 5/19/97 ~ 5/23/97
Abigail Hope Worley ♥ 6/13/09 ~ 4/28/10
Abigale Lynn Nobel ♥ 1/4/11
Adam John Vardon ♥ 8/18/93
Adam Lee Josiah Murphy ♥ 8/05/94 ~ 2/28/06
Adam Michael Encarnacion ♥ 10/24/86 ~ 11/28/02
Adam William Hess ♥ 5/19/85 ~ 9/4/09
Addison Lynn Day ♥ 12/12/10 ~ 4/29/11
Addyson Ryleigh ♥ 2/25/11 ~ 3/5/11
Adin Lee MacPhail ♥ 2/24/07~11/26/08
Adrian Hightower ♥ 10/3/91 ~ 11/26/20
Adrianna May Potts ♥ 11/13/98 ~ 8/29/10
Agnetha Joe-Leighe Revill ♥ 1/3/95 ~ 4/4/96
Aidan Irving Craig ♥ 8/23/96
Aidan Woods ♥ 6/13/80 ~ 7/25/00
Aiden Jones ♥ 4/27/06
Aiden Lee McIver ♥ 12/03/10
Aiden William Thomas ♥ 4/29/09 ~ 2/27/10
Aimee Bird ♥ 8/08/09
Aimee-louise Bates ♥ 10/20/92 ~ 5/16/04
Aishling Marie Roche ♥ 11/18/10 ~ 11/24/10
AJ Markiewicz ♥ 9/5/97 ~ 10/1/97
Aj Timms ♥ 7/12/83 ~ 1/30/06
Akira Mae Gard ♥ 4/11/10 ~ 4/26/10
Alana Boyd-Pollack ♥ 8/4/93 ~ 12/1/11
Alea Grace Frayer ♥ 6/23/06
Aleia Dettmer ♥ 12/7/98 ~ 11/14/10

Aleister Aryan Able Dick ♥ 2/3/11 ~ 3/23/11

Alex "AJ" Owens ♥ 1/3/89 ~ 6/18/13

Alex (Peanut) ♥ 6/30/95 ~ 8/22/12

Alex Daniel Bugenhagen ♥ 3/24/97 ~ 5/31/97

Alex Matheson ♥ 2/17/11 ~ 3/13/11

Alex Simpson ♥ 7/31/07

Alexander F. Farnsworth ♥ 9/5/85 ~ 10/9/10

Alexander Jacob Glant ♥ 10/1/10

Alexander John Whipple ♥ 6/29/09 ~ 4/1/11

Alexander Nicholas Michael Dobbins ♥ 10/1/10 ~ 10/9/10

Alexander Scott Newman ♥ 8/30/11

Alexis Aurora Rave Coleman ♥ 7/4/13 ~ 9/9/13

Alexis Cammile Goudelock ♥ 2/15/07 ~ 4/24/07

Alexis May Harbaugh ♥ 7/8/09 ~ 7/11/10

Alexis Teryn Shaw ♥ 4/12/96 ~ 9/13/09

Alfie James Hone ♥ 11/20/07 ~ 12/28/07

ALia Regina Hughes ♥ 11/13/80 ~ 1/28/13

Alianza Vanessa Garcia ♥ 2/12/94 ~ 6/17/97

Aliza Blay ♥ 6/11/77 ~ 6/10/07

Allison Nicole ♥ 10/99 ~ 6/12

Alton Jess Marshall ♥ 6/3/90 ~ 7/23/09

Alvaro Serna Jr. ♥ 5/24/10

Alyson Bushnell ♥ 1/5/78 ~ 2/20/07

Alyssa Anne Bennett ♥ 12/27/90 ~ 12/24/10

Amanda Brooke Thompson ♥ 2/21/86 ~ 1/30/89

Amanda Elaine Carter ♥ 2/11/88 ~ 4/18/11

Amanda Faith Wooten Forrest ♥ 8/2/03

Amanda Jane Franklin ♥ 1/22/89 ~ 9/26/06

Amanda Louise Clark ♥ 3/19/88 ~ 4/2/07

Amanda Marie Allison ♥ 1/19/93 ~ 1/15/11

Amanda Susan Thierer ♥ 4/28/80 ~ 6/5/07

Amaria Danielle Cook ♥ 9/3/10

Amber Gemma Joyce ♥ 6/16/06

Amber Jean Thompson ♥ 11/15/90 ~ 3/22/09

Amber Lauren (Hays) Vandrey ♥ 1/17/87 ~ 8/16/09

Amber Michelle Kogelis ♥ 4/1/93 ~ 2/25/11

Amber Nicole Davis (Morrison)♥ 1/21/87 ~ 3/8/12

Amelia Louise Keeling ♥ 2/8/08 ~ 3/29/08

Amelia Nancy Field ♥ 9/2/09 ~ 12/21/09

Amiee Marie Luciano ♥ 11/23/91

Amira Justina-Marie Hites ♥ 7/1/10

Amy Louise Turner ♥ 1/31/97 ~ 9/20/09

Analeisa Rose Rivera ♥ 9/21/09 ~ 3/6/11

Andre Jacques Joubert ♥ 7/26/93 ~ 10/4/11

Andre John Archibald ♥ 3/10/11

Andrea Jordan Scherer ♥ 1/30/89~ 1/28/10

Andrew "Andy" John Yeager ♥ 8/74 ~ 4/08

Andrew "Drew" D. Thibodeau ♥ 8/15/78 ~ 9/6/08

Andrew "Yung Pro" Santana ♥ 1/6/93 ~ 10/27/08

Andrew Brinkman ♥ 7/16/90 ~ 7/03/10

Andrew Chard ♥ 2/4/02

Andrew James Black-Matthews ♥ 10/27/06

Andrew James Flick ♥ 12/30/86 ~ 7/8/06

Andrew James Wilson ♥ 12/12/05 ~ 11/07/11

Andrew Justin McPhee ♥ 5/22/97 ~ 12/5/97

Andrew Martin Shoen ♥ 8/23/89 ~ 4/8/11

Andrew Matthew Charles Bransden ♥ 12/20/88 ~ 8/7/10

Andrew Robert John Caul ♥ 4/20/93 ~ 12/8/95

Andrew Scott Wheeler ♥ 9/18/09~10/01/09

Andrew Steven Kellar ♥ 1/20/74 ~ 12/07/93

Andrew Wood ♥ 7/25/74 ~ 12/21/12

Andy Louis Strader III ♥ 8/11/79~ 3/29/80

Angel 2 Morris-Welch ♥ 1/4/06

Angel 3 Morris-Welch ♥ 7/7/06

Angel 4 Morris-Welch ♥ 8/14/07

Angel 5 Morris-Welch ♥ 1/9/10

Angel 6 Morris-Welch ♥ 3/12/10

Angel 7 Morris-Welch ♥ 6/2/11

Angel Anthony Joseph ♥ 12/23/11

Angel Baby Gonzalez-Roldan ♥ 5/2/11

Angel Baby Star ♥ 9/24/05

Angel Baby Twins Fiorino-Baby A♥ 11/14/01;

Baby B ♥ 11/23/01

Angel Chloe Rose Fletcher Parker ♥ 9/11/10~9/11/10

Angel Elaine Craig ♥ 12/19/82 ~ 12/26/82

Angel Gawiuk ♥ 3/16/11

Angel Jack James ♥ 2/14/03

Angel Luis Garcia Jr. ♥ 5/6/75 ~ 8/16/12

Angel Lux Lopez ♥ 6/29/09

Angel Morlok ♥ 5/13/11

Angelica Rae Cartwright ♥ 8/7/95 ~ 6/29/11

Angelina Christine Ramirez. ♥ 8/23/86 ~ 12/13/08

Angelina Lee Escobar ♥ 11/21/89 ~ 9/21/09

Angelito Colula Hernandez ♥ 6/18/10

Angel-Louise Bowers ♥ 11/14/10

Aniyah Hope McKibbin ♥ 8/4/20 ~ 9/12/10

Annie Kate ♥ 6/13/11

Anthony Gee ♥ 8/8/90 ~ 1/28/07

Anthony James Budnack ♥ 3/23/08

Anthony Joseph Mesoraca ♥ 11/01/79~10/03/08

Anthony Joseph Shallo ♥ 2/5/87~10/25/08

Anthony Jr. Richardson ♥ 3/28/89 ~ 8/16/09

Anthony Mason Michael Lancaster ♥ 2/25/74 ~ 9/10/81

Anthony Minutoli ♥ 6/12/92 ~ 7/23/03

Anthony Paul Wodzinski ♥ 1/17/91 ~ 6/10/06

Anthony R. Lamb ♥ 3/9/84 ~ 2/22/10

Anthony Robert Hernandez ♥ 1/14/93 ~ 8/17/09

Anthony Rocco "Rocky" Burton ♥ 3/23/92 ~ 7/05/09

Anthony Victor DeGennaro ♥ 12/2/79 ~ 1/28/97

Anthony Vincent Remshaw ♥ 7/21/75 ~ 7/23/98

April Lynn Brooks ♥ 4/3/96 ~ 5/13/10

April Michelle Pera ♥ 8/2/88~8/7/07

Archie Liam Hopkinson ♥ 7/4/09

Arial Elizbeth Thomas ♥ 12/16/09

Aria-Storm Carey ♥ 6/30/06

Arik Thomas Riddle ♥ 7/29/10

Ashlee Nicole Drouillard ♥ 5/9/95 ~ 11/15/09

Ashlei Rose Walker ♥ 4/11/01 ~ 4/27/01

Ashleigh Anne Love ♥ 9/17/90 ~ 10/6/09

Ashleigh Christine Mauseth ♥ 3/10/92 ~ 9/28/07

Ashleigh Diane Jacobs ♥ 5/3/85 ~ 3/10/12

Ashley Allison Lynch ♥ 2/10/85

Ashley Breann Burchett ♥ 11/9/00 ~ 12/26/00

Ashley Lena Sutton ♥ 8/4/85 ~ 6/7/10

Ashley Marie Martin ♥ 12/16/92 ~ 2/18/13

Ashley Marie O'Kelley ♥ 12/11/96 ~ 11/22/97

Ashley Nicole Stuart ♥ 5/14/89 ~6/25/07

Ashley Remark ♥ 3/8/07 ~ 4/21/07
Ashley Savannah ♥ 7/9/06
Ashlie Duit ♥ 12/21/87 ~ 2/13/09
Ashlyn Breanna Poole ♥ 7/31/90 ~ 1/23/12
Ashton and Kane King ♥ 3/25/08
Aubrey Elaine Cowger ♥ 11/20/89 ~ 3/18/93
Aubrey Skye ♥ 8/22/10
Audrina E Escano ♥ 5/25/91 ~ 12/20/09
Aurora Nicole Pruett ♥ 9/10/09
Austin Clark Zahn ♥ 7/20/06 ~ 7/23/06
Austin James Henry ♥ 11/17/01 ~ 8/22/09
Austin Leonard Launderville ♥ 10/6/90 ~ 2/3/13
Autum Nichole Meeks ♥ 12/18/95~ 2/21/96
Ava and Patrick Scheffler ♥ 6/25/09
Baby Bean ♥ 11/24/06
Baby J. Monzon ♥ 10/20/10
Baby Prince Peter ♥ 2/9/11 ~ 2/13/11
Baker Andrew Troxler ♥ 2/5/11 ~ 4/7/11
Barry Geesey ♥ 4/30/79 ~ 2/18/06
Barry John ♥ 1983 ~ 2009
Baylee Michelle Heblon ♥ 1/30/04 ~ 10/31/04
Benjamin Akira Yatsu ♥ 12/13/95~ 7/10/11
Benjamin Alan Stricklin ♥ 10/3/84 ~ 4/28/00
Benjamin Jarred Chanin ♥ 6/12/94 ~7/26/10
Benjamin Stricklin ♥ 10/3/84 ~ 4/28/00
Bernadette Dawn Ingram ♥ 8/08/84~7/26/09
Blaine Arthur Stoner ♥ 4/13/10
Blake Anthony Callender ♥ 8/14/09 ~ 8/18/09
Blake Easter-Marsh ♥ 12/4/11 ~ 2/13/12
Blake Edward Sobeck ♥ 11/18/84 ~ 11/8/10
Blake Vaughn ♥ 4/21/88 ~ 8/22/13
Bobbie Lynn Wilks ♥ 4/16/88 ~ 10/29/07
Bobby Haight ♥ 10/1/74 ~ 6/16/94
Bobby Shawn Beer ♥ 11/29/82 ~ 3/23/06
Brack Harrison ♥ 12/4/80 ~ 6/13/84
Brad Downs ♥ 7/4/86 ~ 10/6/07
Bradley James Langley ♥ 3/18/91 ~ 4/25/09
Bradley Ryan Place ♥ 8/7/07 ~ 9/14/07
Branden "Bubby" Runion ♥ 6/5/89 ~ 10/20/12

Brandi Lee Hagel ♥ 6/7/76 ~ 2/5/96
Brandi Lynn Mitchell-Edwards. ♥ 2/20/78 ~ 9/17/07
Brandi Lynn Smith ♥ 9/16/83 ~ 7/18/09
Brandon Alan Garcia ♥ 4/24/91~1/5/10
Brandon Austin Letsche ♥ 3/9/95 ~ 8/6/13
Brandon Beckley ♥ 4/21/83~4/14/07
Brandon David Goudie ♥ 6/2/05 ~ 8/17/10
Brandon Dewayne Martin ♥ 12/16/92 ~ 8/2/08
Brandon James Higgins ♥ 9/19/89 ~ 3/20/13
Brandon Lee Bricker ♥ 1/15/97 ~ 7/10/06
Brandon Lee McGlothlin ♥ 12/31/88 ~ 5/21/11
Brandon Lee McWilliams ♥ 6/17/93 ~4/30/10
Brandon Matthew Goodpaster ♥ 5/14/94 ~ 9/8/10
Brandon Michael Whitby ♥ 1/22/86~08/21/08
Brandon Mitchell Harrison-Douglas ♥ 6/3/94 ~ 2/18/06
Brandon Phillip Talbert ♥ 3/26/92 ~ 4/8/11
Brandon Robert Harris ♥ 11/14/04 ~ 12/11/11
Brandon Tyler Beshada ♥ 3/21/1982 ~ 4/1/07
Brandon Wade Barnett ♥ 1/28/10
Brayden Russell Zieg ♥ 1/5/07 ~ 6/6/08
Breanne and Brennae Harjo ♥ 6/6/08
Brendan Samuel Ward ♥ 9/26/01 ~ 9/27/01
Brenden Louis Lowenberg ♥ 3/9/85 ~ 2/15/12
Brenden Reese Spring ♥ 2/22/92
Brett Randall Jaynes ♥ 12/24/88~5/24/11
Brian "BeeKay" Kerr ♥ 2/3/92 ~ 3/26/11
Brian "Bubba" Paul Bowling ♥ 5/01/81 ~ 10/19/96
Brian Andrew Wentworth ♥ 1/10/95 ~ 3/6/10
Brian Balzer ♥ 12/9/86 ~ 10/29/09
Brian Charles Ernst ♥ 3/11/91 ~ 3/16/10
Brian Edward Clark ♥ 9/20/90 ~ 6/21/08
Brian Eldridge ♥ 5/14/80 ~ 9/5/13
Brian Eric ♥ 10/6/69 ~ 12/21/12
Brian Frederick Perrault ♥ 8/27/93 ~ 12/1/06
Briana Becerra ♥ 3/18/02 ~ 1/26/10
Brianna Allen ♥ 12/11/99 ~ 5/22/00
Brianna Emily Silliker ♥ 1/4/94 ~ 11/4/10
Brianna Renee Rogers ♥ 12/11/99 ~ 5/22/00
Brice Connel Parsons ♥ 3/20/11 ~ 3/27/11

Brigit Elizabeth McGee ♥ 10/24/00 ~ 10/26/00
Britni Nicole Jaynes ♥ 5/8/87~11/26/87
Brittany M. Jenkins ♥ 8/26/94 ~ 1/20/03
Brittany Nicole Thomas ♥ 3/12/88 ~2/27/10
Brooke Gemma Mayon ♥ 6/18/09
Brooke Sierra Fleming ♥ 2/26/01
Brooklyn Gladun ♥ 6/7/11
Bryan Christopher Plunkett ♥ 1/12/85 ~ 10/28/02
Bryan Keith Gamble ♥ 5/18/97 ~ 5/22/97
Byron Mallett ♥ 2/10/00 ~ 8/22/13
Byron Reid Clink ♥ 8/17/10
Cade James Bailey ♥ 10/17/00 ~ 9/21/10
Caden Jorden Ansin ♥ 10/03/06 ~ 2/23/11
Cailou Boswell ♥ 4/8/10
Caleb Burne King ♥ 4/6/11
Caleb Michael Wiesen ♥ 6/1/11
Callum John Gorton ♥ 4/21/09 ~ 8/7/09
Cameron Robert Wolfe ♥ 11/5/04
Camillie M. White ♥ 3/7/04 ~ 6/25/04
Camryn Lee Shultz ♥ 10/29/11 ~ 10/27/13
Candice Hynes ♥ 8/26/98
Cara Marie Holley ♥ 8/19/91 ~ 7/7/10
Carl Joathon Lambert ♥ 3/12/82 ~ 1/23/02
Carliser M Rodriquez ♥ 11/27/74 ~ 1/31/10
Carston Wayne Kownack ♥ 11/17/03 ~ 8/1/08
Casey Alexander Stricker ♥ 12/18/01 ~ 9/24/11
Casey Beals ♥ 4/13/90 ~ 1/18/13
Casey Faye Marie Aschan-Cox ♥ 4/8/92 ~ 3/18/10
Casey Luffman ♥ 2/27/90 ~ 4/6/09
Casey Michele Costello ♥ 7/25/91 ~ 9/21/91
Casey Nicole Pannochia ♥ 6/10/89 ~3/23/09
Cassandra Baker ♥ 4/5/85 ~ 8/10/08
Cassandra Goeddel ♥ 4/24/82 ~ 8/15/13
Cassidy Joy Andel ♥ 10/26/94 ~ 11/4/10
Cassie Elizabeth Myers ♥ 12/23/97 ~ 9/30/02
Cayden Wince ♥ 12/12/94 ~ 1/31/07
Cayleb Ralph-Joseph ♥ 8/1/00
Cayliss Treahn Mothershed ♥ 12/1/93 ~ 11/14/11
Cecilia Kay Balma ♥ 1/5/06 ~ 4/7/09

Cerridwyn "Kerry" Maire Ursula Brigid Roseanne Lujan ♥
5/17/89 ~ 5/20/08
Chad Michael, Madison Marie and Bailey Jean Horton ♥
9/11/09
Chanel Peckham. ♥ 6/30/08 ~ 4/6/10
Chaos David-Michael Hotes ♥ 1/12/11
Charlene Ashley Maloney ♥ 7/11/92 ~ 5/16/12
Charlene Whitethread ♥ 5/26/81
Charles Alan Williams ♥ 8/7/90 ~ 12/17/09
Charles Daniel Hillhouse ♥ 8/28/86 ~ 8/28/08
Charles Patrick Mottram ♥ 1/18/88~7/13/10
Charles Vincent Michael Agricola ♥ 4/14/89 ~ 10/19/07
Charlie Jack Grady ♥ 3/27/10
Charlie Kelly ♥ 3/16/70 ~ 7/11/99
Charlotte Elise Walker ♥ 3/14/98 ~ 2/20/08
Chase Cameron Cummings ♥ 10/9/93 ~ 9/18/12
Chase Christopher Wright ♥ 7/10/10
Chaun Dale Lambert ♥ 7/11/76 ~ 9/21/00
Chelsea Ann Morgan ♥ 3/16/94
Chelsea Lynn Munson ♥ 1/18/90 ~ 2/11/12
Chelsea R. Murphy ♥ 3/18/92 ~ 3/4/08
Chene Engelbrecht ♥ 3/11/87 ~ 10/7/91
Cheyanne Karen Audet ♥ 10/13/80 ~ 10/27/11
Cheyenne Anjelica Decker (Jackson) ♥ 11/19/94
Cheyenne Haines ♥ 9/26/86 ~ 4/27/10
Chris Gerlt Jr. ♥ 8/78 ~ 11/98
Chriss Therron Smith ♥ 4/18/74
Chrissy Emmons ♥ 5/6/85 ~ 1/17/10
Christian Cade Lowery ♥ 1/4/97 ~ 9/15/08
Christian Frechette ♥ 10/17/02 ~ 7/13/07
Christian Sain Livingston ♥ 8/9/10
Christian Sean Jorgensen ♥ 12/9/77 ~ 1/18/10
Christian Taelor and Austyn Shane ♥ 4/11/98
Christian Webb ♥ 11/30/08 ~ 12/2/08
Christina Marie Smith ♥ 5/15/87 ~ 2/6/12
Christina Stellato ♥ 10/14/80 ~ 8/17/10
Christopher "Chit" Amedee ♥ 11/4/93 ~ 2/19/09
Christopher "Chris" L. Stiles. ♥ 1/18/84 ~ 6/20/10
Christopher "CJ" John Wheatley ♥ 1/26/85 ~ 1/1/10

Christopher "Critter" Joseph Smith ♥ 12/11/97 ~ 4/21/11
Christopher Allen Reinhardt ♥ 10/4/08 ~ 10/3/07
Christopher Bolduc ♥ 8/20/90 ~ 7/23/02
Christopher Bynum Younts ♥ 8/7/03 ~ 12/20/03
Christopher Charles "Charlie" Gordon ♥ 12/13/00 ~ 12/7/09
Christopher Collins ♥ 4/19/75
Christopher Dafoe ♥ 11/15/82 ~ 10/6/07
Christopher E. (Burger) Barski ♥ 10/30/78 ~ 3/25/13
Christopher Josef Locke ♥ 11/7/06 ~ 12/17/06
Christopher Karamitros ♥ 1/13/82 ~ 1/6/10
Christopher Kessler ♥ 6/16/78
Christopher Proctor ♥ 12/29/81 ~ 5/13/98
Christopher R.Garner ♥ 8/17/90 ~ 4/12/92
Christopher Robert Swartz ♥ 7/11/80 ~ 8/29/10
Christopher Sansome ♥ 8/19/69~8/29/69
Christopher Shane Jones ♥ 6/14/89 ~ 9/3/89
Christopher Wayne Heath ♥ 6/10/88 ~ 12/10/09
Cian JonRichard McCorkle ♥ 11/14/07 ~ 11/28/09
Claire Elizabeth Stroud ♥ 10/26/11
Clay Ellis ♥ 6/13/93 ~ 8/23/94
Clint Wheatley ♥ 6/9/78 ~ 8/27/02
Clinton Terry Milam ♥ 4/07/93 ~ 8/05/03
Cody Adam Acton ♥ 5/18/90 ~ 10/16/10
Cody Dean Field ♥ 3/16/95 ~ 7/3/95
Cody Michael Green ♥ 1/22/89 ~ 2/9/09
Cody Ray Scarbrough ♥ 7/2/02 ~ 4/28/09
Cole Chandler Gray ♥ 10/5/05
Colin Matthew Scott Ingham ♥ 12/14/09 ~ 12/28/09
Colin Michael "Mike" Ewers ♥ 12/18/81 ~ 6/21/03
Colleen Marie Douglass ♥ 5/12/61 ~ 5/18/92
Collin Xavier Coloura ♥ 4/18/11
Collins Randall Huffman ♥ 5/18/11 ~ 5/19/11
Colton Hunter Perry Hopkins ♥ 5/7/99 ~ 12/5/04
Conner and Kennedy ♥ 7/24/09
Connor James and Collin Michael Conklin ♥ 10/14/10
Conor Nelson Tye ♥ 12/76 ~ 6/09
Cooper Douglas Stulz ♥ 10/15/01 ~ 4/13/10
Cooper John Mayon ♥ 4/20/07
Corey Andrew Evans ♥ 10/1/87 ~ 11/19/09

Corey Christopher Goad ♥ 8/13/87

Corrinna Marie Romero ♥ 7/3/73 ~ 5/21/04

Courtney "Blondie" Ann Koehler ♥ 5/24/94 ~ 8/16/07

Courtney "Boo" Rae Miller ♥ 9/17/97 ~ 11/13/10

Courtney Jane Houldey ♥ 8/10/01

Craig G. Lewtas ♥ 10/7/70 ~ 7/28/09

Craig Michael Copsey ♥ 6/02/80 ~ 10/08/08

Craig R. Bresson ♥ 1/08/85 ~ 11/26/06

Craig Steven Doubt III ♥ 9/30/89 ~ 9/8/08

Crawford Alan Carnahan ♥ 8/21/88 ~ 5/12/07

Crystal Mae Lopez ♥ 11/18/76 ~ 11/20/09

Curt B. Allred Jr. ♥ 6/26/76 ~ 1/16/09

Curtis Charles Lewis ♥ 5/26/70 ~ 6/20/06

Daisha Rosemary Rogers ♥ 4/5/94 ~ 11/27/94

Dakota Shane Casey ♥ 12/31/91 ~ 1/12/92

Dakota Wayne Hoffman-Bennett ♥ 2/23/02 ~ 1/29/11

Dakotah Rayne Dougherty ♥ 7/7/99 ~ 9/6/99

Dallas Orion Caswell-Snyder ♥ 1/1/05

Dalton Lee Davis ♥ 11/2/56 ~1/22/89

Dameon S. Norman ♥ 12/17/70 ~ 4/12/06

Damian John Richardson ♥ 10/31/83 ~ 11/15/02

Damian Kent ♥ 10/28/92 ~ 11/27/10

Damien Joseph Brian Hordell ♥ 12/9/07 ~ 4/22/08

Damien Michael Gorse ♥ 10/20/01 ~ 11/6/01

Damir Geovanny Baker ♥ 7/16/11

Dan Kelley ♥ 6/18/75 ~ 10/2/08

Dana Richard Cackowski ♥ 9/18/84 ~ 10/2/09

Daniel Anthony Patterson ♥ 4/9/95 ~ 3/10/98

Daniel Aust ♥ 7/7/76 ~ 8/9/03

Daniel Clark Gale ♥ 5/5/94 ~ 3/8/10

Daniel J Martinez ♥ 8/7/77 ~ 7/5/11

Daniel Jadon Pruett ♥ 12/12/04

Daniel James Amar ♥ 10/08/85 ~ 7/24/97

Daniel Joseph Whisler ♥ 12/11/70 ~ 6/27/09

Daniel Matthew Imhoff ♥ 6/11/88 ~ 12/18/10

Daniel N. Krehbiel ♥ 5/6/96 ~ 11/28/08

Daniel P. Kelley ♥ 6/18/75 ~ 10/2/08

Daniel Ronk ♥ 3/15/91 ~ 4/7/10

Daniel Steven ♥ 1/02/11

Daniel Tanner Gehrman ♥ 3/2/13 ~ 3/2/13
Daniel Walsh ♥ 11/8/83 ~ 7/15/02
Daniel-Alexander ♥ 2/15/97 ~ 7/25/74
Danielle Louise Keelan ♥ 7/11/90 ~ 8/31/09
Danielle N. Trevithick. ♥ 6/28/88 ~ 8/12/10
Danielle Pauline Murphy ♥ 5/26/81 ~ 1/29/06
Danny Bo Mei ♥ 5/17/10
Danny DeSantis Jr. ♥ 8/07/67 ~ 9/10/05
Danny James Gominsky ♥ 8/12/58 ~ 2/20/12
Danny Watson Jr. ♥ 8/16/73 ~ 4/25/04
Dante Avery Nathaniel Milford ♥ 8/27/97 ~ 11/12/97
Darien M. Wilson ♥ 4/29/83 ~ 1/4/06
Daris J. Shields ♥ 11/28/80 ~ 11/03/10
Darren Grant ♥ 3/31/73 ~ 12/21/07
Darren Junior Marsh ♥ 2/13/06 ~ 5/5/06
Darren Marsh ♥ 9/6/83 ~ 10/28/05
Dauson Alijah Bim Peace ♥ 2/24/05 ~ 5/26/06
David August Cardenas ♥ 7/7/98 ~ 11/10/10
David Duanne Rouse ♥ 7/10/88 ~ 8/20/08
David Dustin Finch ♥ 11/30/86 ~ 12/8/10
David Edward Maclay ♥ 11/26/03 ~ 7/19/11
David Jay Kestner ♥ 5/14/93
David Jordan Bachner ♥ 1/16/91 ~ 8/11/09
David Mark Vitiello Jr. ♥ 3/27/89 ~ 11/06/08
David Michael Russell ♥ 7/23/02
David Thomas Snow ♥ 6/15/09
Dawn M. (Paul) Reynolds ♥ 1/14/74 ~ 12/08/09
Dawn Marie Miller ♥ 6/9/70 ~ 10/22/92
Debbie Unruh ♥ 5/30/85 ~ 8/7/07
Debbie V. Kern ♥ 10/17/70 ~ 1/25/92
DebbieAnn Palmeri ♥ 3/10/85 ~ 3/14/85
Dennis Anthony Farr ♥ 2/9/87 ~ 3/6/11
Denver Ray Stubrich ♥ 7/14/97
Derek Christopher Mackay ♥ 8/5/87 ~ 9/15/08
Derrick Bradley Stubrich ♥ 7/22/83 ~ 3/10/13
Destiny Ann-Maureen Chesebro ♥ 5/3/11
Destiny Marie Cissell ♥ 5/4/99 ~ 10/27/09
Devan Christopher White ♥ 5/11/95 ~ 1/7/11
Devin Jacob McKibbin ♥ 7/28/09

Devin Taylor Johnson ♥ 7/22/91 ~ 11/5/10
Devon Daniel Morrison ♥ 11/1/02 ~ 9/14/13
Devon James Kushman ♥ 10/27/04
Dillon Ray Jett ♥ 1/15/87 ~ 5/09/10
Dino Valentino Raponi ♥ 6/2/77 ~ 1/20/07
Dominick Jason Barajas ♥ 12/19/92 ~ 12/19/10
Dominik Luke Pinzone ♥ 4/03/85 ~ 12/13/05
Don Glen Thornhill ♥ 5/6/93 ~ 8/22/09
Donald W. Craig ♥ 1/8/35 ~ 2/8/82
Donaway Shylow Rego ♥ 5/23/88 ~ 10/24/09
Dorothy Dawn Palmer ♥ 3/14/91 ~ 11/3/07
Doug Hess ♥ 1/12/96 ~ 7/28/13
Dustin Koby Wunderlich ♥ 4/19/84 ~ 3/13/13
Dustin L. Hooten ♥ 7/1/84 ~ 10/14/02
Dustin Lovett ♥ 6/15/81 ~ 4/7/05
Dustin Ross Murphy ♥ 9/24/85 ~ 4/15/10
Dustin Wayne Plyler ♥ 11/27/03
Dylan and Evan Lima Pechilis ♥ 7/19/07
Dylan James George ♥ 11/8/91 ~ 9/2/12
Dylan Kirby Montgomery ♥ 2/24/10 ~ 2/24/10
Dylan Markwell ♥ 12/19/05 ~ 12/24/05
Dylan Patrick Major ♥ 12/4/81 ~ 12/4/81
Eddie Porrazzo ♥ 10/31/71 ~ 1/15/10
Edmund Thomas Roland ♥ 7/10/86 ~ 7/10/07
Eduardo "Eddy" Jorge Triana ♥ 5/15/75 ~ 4/13/11
Eilidh Beth Simpson ♥ 9/24/10
Elias Michael Cole ♥ 9/30/08 ~ 10/15/08
Elijah "Eli" Xavier Elmore ♥ 10/7/10 ~ 12/14/10
Elijah Manuel Eilets ♥ 6/10/03
Elijah Seth Moye ♥ 12/15/81 ~ 1/5/01
Elijah Zaine Caro Cooper ♥ 5/11/01 ~ 10/12/08
Elin Marianne Ossiander ♥ 6/3/10
Elisa Mendez ♥ 3/10/83 ~ 8/13/12
Elisabeth Evelyn Allread ♥ 8/11/83 ~ 8/24/08
Elizabeth Hudson ♥ 5/20/87 ~ 4/11/08
Elizabeth Paige Cornes ♥ 8/14/96 ~ 2/25/07
Ellen Rose Floyd (McGuiggan) ♥ 8/23/92 ~ 4/4/10
Elliana Alyssa Zaidel ♥ 7/18/05 ~ 7/13/07
Ellie Brooke Wilkinson ♥ 3/5/07 ~ 1/25/11

Emilee Skye and Dylen Jacob Hummel ♥ 11/18/11
Emily & Emilio Garcia ♥ 2/25/93
Emily Lynn Brown and unborn child ♥ 8/8/82 ~ 1/15/09
Emily Mae Martin ♥ 9/19/00 ~ 7/16/01
Emily Rose Ford ♥ 9/28/10 ~ 10/10/10
Emma Christine Thomas ♥ 4/10/08 ~ 9/18/09
Emma Frances Dalton ♥ 9/22/10 ~ 4/17/11
Emma Louise Jessop ♥ 12/31/87 ~ 8/29/10
Emma Stephens Armstrong ♥ 2/12/09 ~ 2/15/10
Enrique "Ricky" Lopez, Jr ♥ 1/12/89 ~ 7/30/10
Ephraim David Schultz ♥ 7/19/83 ~ 5/12/05
Eric Anthony Dyke ♥ 3/30/81 ~ 11/4/06
Eric Hargrave ♥ 8/17/83 ~ 11/04/08
Eric John Simco ♥ 10/4/81 ~ 7/28/08
Eric Nicholas Irby ♥ 5/28/87 ~ 5/4/11
Eric Partin ♥ 1/20/87 ~ 5/30/10
Eric Ronald Schwed ♥ 9/6/87 ~ 9/8/97
Eric Ryan Dudley ♥ 10/12/1984 ~ 11/05/11
Erica Sellers ♥ 5/5/90 ~ 8/9/09
Erika Joy Rowan ♥ 9/23/91 ~ 2/25/08
Erika Kelly Anstett ♥ 3/12/82 ~ 2/18/03
Ernest Richard Farris ♥ 10/8/92
Ernesto Rojo Jr. ♥ 10/21/11 ~ 8/14/13
Ethan Carter Lane ♥ 3/12/10 ~ 6/4/10
Ethan Cody Bleu Saltar ♥ 12/15/93 ~ 9/19/10
Evelyn Cheryl Chadwick-Sawyer ♥ 3/17/11
Faith Fogarty ♥ 10/13/99
Felipe Catalan ♥ 8/24/85 ~ 10/28/06
Feodora Laurent Kushman ♥10/31/08
Finlay John Houlding ♥ 9/5/10
Franchesca Mercedese Rowell ♥ 3/3/97
Frankie Aaron Gallimore ♥ 7/25/88 ~ 10/8/08
Freddie Endres ♥ 8/05/97 ~ 8/02/10
Gabriel Lopez ♥ 7/23/81 ~ 7/23/05
Gage Scott Williams ♥ 8/4/10
Garrett James Smith ♥ 9/24/92 ~ 5/15/10
Gavin Matthew King ♥ 6/3/87 ~ 8/14/09
Gemma Keely Mayon ♥ 1/11/08
Genoveva Soriano Salazar ♥ 9/22/57 ~ 11/12/82

Geoffrey P. Edwards ♥ 5/6/84 ~ 5/22/02
George Patrick Joseph Gamblin III ♥ 1/28/84 ~ 7/26/10
George-Paul Webb ♥ 4/10/92
Georgia Elise Douglass ♥ 5/2/02 ~ 1/21/05
Gerrit Storm ♥ 7/9/91 ~ 11/28/98
Gian Leo A. Combalicer ♥ 10/6/13 ~ 10/11/13
Grace Samantha Mayri Hilbert. ♥ 3/17/11
Gracie Stultz ♥ 1/27/10
Gracie-Rose Lane ♥ 12/6/10 ~ 12/6/10
Gregory Edward Whale Jr. ♥ 9/2/91 ~ 4/26/10
Gunnar Hosia Dougherty ♥ 4/27/98
Hailey Nevaeh'Lea Stolz ♥ 4/28/06 ~ 8/22/06
Hailey Nicole Larsen ♥ 12/23/08 ~ 7/28/10
Hannah Gerlt ♥ 7/3/03 ~ 7/17/10
Harley Davidson Bivens ♥ 7/15/87 ~ 6/19/05
Harley Jay Fox ♥ 4/25/01 ~ 6/10/08
Harlow Elizabeth Schaefer ♥ 5/21/11 ~ 6/15/11
Harold W. Smith, Jr. ♥ 5/23/74 ~ 3/28/10
Harvey Dylan Merchant ♥ 9/7/07
Hayden Allen Kimbell ♥ 3/20/10
Hayden Andrew ♥ 1/17/04
Hayley Patricia Aird ♥ 6/24/10 ~ 6/28/10
Heather Brookshire ♥ 4/13/81 ~ 5/21/08
Heather Corinn Schwartz ♥ 10/12/90 ~ 10/28/09
Heather Lynn Russell ♥ 7/28/79 ~ 5/4/09
Heidi Lynn Crawford ♥ 8/18/89
Henry William Berlin ♥ 2/23/06 ~ 7/22/08
Hollie Michelle Battershill ♥ 4/21/01
Hope Elna Lockhart ♥ 11/19/10
Hubert George Rose 4th ♥ 12/19/78 ~ 7/15/12
Hunnie Beth Lance ♥ 12/26/79 ~ 10/8/09
Ian James Foster ♥ 11/10/77 ~ 9/8/06
Ian Thomas Kosky ♥ 6/11/80 ~ 10/15/10
Ieisha Pipon Doreen Coulineur ♥ 1/10/98 ~ 4/21/11
Isaac Marvin-Lee Stokes ♥ 2/12/03
Isabel Martins ♥ 7/25/97 ~ 3/10/11
Isabel Simone Fiorino ♥ 5/2/03 ~ 12/17/05
Isabella Faith Karol ♥ 8/23/11
Isabella Marie Crispino ♥ 1/12/10

Isabella Maybre Kinard ♥ 12/26/10
Isaiah M. Alonso ♥ 4/26/04 ~ 9/10/10
Isaiah Matthew Mangum ♥ 10/22/98
Ishmal-joshua Thomas ♥ 12/4/04
Itty and Bitty Lux Lopez ♥ 6/22/01
Izaya Michael Baiz ♥ 8/12/03 ~ 11/27/08
J. Grant Lewis ♥ 12/19/79 ~ 1/17/06
J. Michael Brooksher ♥ 8/19/89 ~ 12/12/11
Jack Greg Reynolds-McCourt ♥ 7/23/10
Jack James Dickey ♥ 4/7/98 ~ 6/15/06
Jack L. Garner ♥ 12/13/67 ~ 11/18/11
Jackilynn Rainn Stoermer ♥ 5/15/04 ~ 6/6/04
Jacklyn Christine Hoover ♥ 1/20/92 ~ 8/28/11
Jacob "Jake" Alexander-Lee Gagnon ♥ 5/1/03 ~ 9/25/08
Jacob "Jake" Anthony Perez ♥ 7/20/98 ~ 12/17/09
Jacob Kyle Johnson ♥ 11/19/83 ~ 11/26/97
Jacob Laurence Geiser ♥ 5/17/06 ~ 1/15/08
Jacob Michael Scott McLeod-Steinmetz ♥ 6/17/91 ~ 6/16/05
Jacob Ryan Yergeau ♥ 9/25/99 ~ 9/25/99
Jacob Michael Nelson ♥ 10/18/08 ~ 5/20/12
Jade BoRam Mebane ♥ 9/24/95 ~ 3/22/12
Jadra Hawkins ♥ 1/9/09
Jaiden John Page ♥ 2/4/11
Jaime Patton Daugherty ♥ 10/1/09
Jaise Michael Taylor 'Bear' ♥ 8/3/08 ~ 9/29/10
Jakylar Leon Burns ♥ 10/5/08 ~ 2/2/11
Jamal Thomas "Tommy" EL-Ferkh ♥ 5/8/08
James "Jamie" W. McCombs Jr. ♥ 2/12/73 ~ 5/12/98.
James "Jay" Heath Jr. ♥ 10/7/87 ~ 3/8/09
James Amato Jr. ♥ 1/10/86 ~ 10/03/10
James Brandon Smith ♥ 1/18/80 ~ 7/29/02
James Jeffrey Burnette ♥ 1/14/76 ~ 6/18/08
James L. Peterson ♥ 4/6/80 ~ 3/19/07
James L. Vandewater IV ♥ 1/28/86 ~ 11/3/07
James Melford Young III ♥ 1/29/91 ~ 8/6/09
James Raymond Knowles ♥ 12/1/88 ~ 3/25/89
James Reid Clink ♥ 8/17/10
James Thomas Castaneda ♥ 10/2/08
James Thomas Galanti-Smith ♥ 2/23/10

James Thomas Grose ♥ 3/9/76 ~ 12/27/07
James Thomas Price ♥ 3/24/96 ~ 11/1/96
Jamie Lyons ♥ 2/23/90 ~ 2/25/90
Jarod Alan Scott ♥ 3/23/81 ~ 9/19/09
Jaron Keith Morgan ♥ 8/31/89 ~6/27/12
Jason C. Cooper ♥ 9/21/78 ~ 4/30/04
Jason Christopher Moore ♥ 5/24/72 ~ 3/17/11
Jason Daniello ♥ 9/26/97 ~ 7/24/11
Jason Frank Meyers ♥ 3/18/85 ~ 3/22/09
Jason Gray Thompson ♥ 8/24/80 ~ 10/13/07
Jason James Olinger ♥ 4/20/71 ~ 12/17/11
Jason Lee Webb ♥ 3/28/76 ~ 9/21/92
Jason M. Burke ♥ 5/5/75 ~ 11/30/01
Jason Patrick N.Infante ♥ 7/2/94 ~ 8/12/12
Jason Phillip Brooks ♥ 10/18/84 ~ 8/8/10
Jason Ray Peyton ♥ 11/01/94 ~ 4/28/11
Jason Robert Maddox ♥ 11/17/09 ~ 11/22/09
Jaxson Benjamin Norton ♥ 10/31/06 ~ 3/30/11
Jay Garrison ♥ 10/93
Jayden Blake Schneider ♥ 1/15/11
Jaydin Lamont ♥ 10/18/03
Jayjay Howard Donovan ♥ 4/06/09
Jaylib JaQai Butler ♥ 5/9/05 ~ 9/28/05
Jaz'myn Marie Buress ♥ 8/18/13 ~ 10/8/13
Jeff King ♥ 9/18/74 ~ 3/11/11
Jeffrey Call ♥ 8/9/99~1/17/11
Jeffrey T. Felix ♥ 11/30/72 ~ 1/29/99
Jema Michelle Harjo ♥ 4/12/09
Jennifer Alyson Bushnell ♥ 1/5/78 ~ 2/20/07.
Jennifer Ann Greenwald ♥ 10/24/81 ~ 3/16/98
Jennifer E. Chaffin-Kinnee ♥ 9/14/73 ~ 1/14/13
Jennifer Jane Metcalfe ♥ 11/6/85 ~ 2/8/10
Jennifer Lynn Rider ♥ 4/28/86 ~ 8/24/12
Jennifer Michelle Banks ♥ 6/4/76 ~ 7/27/00
Jenny Lynn Morris ♥ 5/4/79 ♥ 12/4/96
Jeremiah Isaac Deskins ♥ 9/21/07~1/12/08
Jeremy "Worm" Lawson ♥ 5/3/86 ~ 2/14/10
Jeremy Andrew Barnes ♥ 11/23/80 ~ 9/8/98
Jeremy Austin Wagner ♥ 8/18/00 ~ 9/5/00

Jeremy Jayson Marshall ♥ 4/26/75 ~ 9/10/01
Jeremy Lee Ward ♥ 12/31/86 ~ 3/23/09
Jeremy Lynn Alcorn ♥ 11/8/86 ~ 6/15/09
Jeremy Paul Karrer ♥ 1/25/80 ~ 1/7/87
Jeremy Reece Foote ♥ 8/14/88 ~ 1/27/10
Jeremy Robert Smith ♥ 11/21/71 ~ 5/31/10
Jermey Dee Gill ♥ 6/8/83 ~ 10/25/05
Jerry "Junior" Stevens II ♥ 8/7/91 ~ 7/18/09
Jerry Darren Austin ♥ 12/29/82 ~ 4/16/83
Jerry Torres ♥ 2/7/85 ~ 11/14/03
Jesse B Gatts ♥ 5/16/95 ~ 3/30/11
Jesse James McEathron ♥ 9/13/90 ~ 3/18/09
Jesse Lockamy ♥ 4/18/83 ~ 11/17/99
Jesse Voinski ♥ 2/23/80 ~ 5/12/08
Jessica Danielle Herrington ♥ 1/15/92 ~ 1/20/09
Jessica Gorcham ♥ 6/23/06
Jessica Grenier ♥ 5/31/83 ~ 1/22/11
Jessica Kate Willrich ♥ 2/6/82 ~ 8/28/06
Jessica Marie Gleason ♥ 3/7/82 ~ 2/22/05
Jessica Pirkel ♥ 6/16/85 ~ 6/19/87
Jesus Guadalupe Rios ♥ 6/5/13
Jethro James ♥ 3/10/11 ~ 3/10/11
Jill Marie Gregory ♥ 3/16/73 ~ 8/14/08
Jimma Gabrelle Cape-Kiser ♥ 6/16/02 ~ 9/19/09
Jimmie Andrew Hawkins ♥ 4/7/84 ~ 10/6/11
Joe Elliot ♥ 8/13/99
Joe Keel ♥ 6/1/80 ~ 4/10/13
Joe King ♥ 7/3/63 ~ 11/18/05
Joey Scarpa ♥ 9/13/71 ~ 3/20/95
John Andrew Hall ♥ 10/6/71 ~ 7/1/10
John Edward Pegan IV ♥ 7/29/10 ~ 8/20/10
John Jacob Thomas Richey ♥ 4/3/88 ~ 6/19/05
John Michael Delehanty ♥ 1/25/88 ~ 11/1/08
John Michael McConnell ♥ 3/23/10 ~ 4/30/10
John Paul Hughes ♥ 10/3/89 ~ 8/7/07
John Paul Smith ♥ 3/20/95 ~ 12/14/04
John Tartagia Jr. ♥ 11/22/82 ~ 8/13/05
John Travis Gordon ♥ 2/11/73 ~ 5/18/08
John Wayne Corcoran ♥ 7/10/98 ~ 10/9/09

Johnathan M. Burns ♥ 1/8/83 ~ 11/17/00
John-Benjamin Bohannon ♥ 4/7/87 ~ 12/24/08
Johnna Giordano ♥ 2/12/93 ~ 12/24/10
Johnnie Derden ♥ 11/17/66 ~ 10/2/04
Johnny Bob Moore ♥ 10/4/71 ~ 9/18/13
Johnny Eddy Potter ♥ 12/12/06 ~ 12/14/06
Jonah Alexander Cullett ♥ 2/24/94 ~ 5/23/10
Jonah Chen Glovsky ♥ 12/16/96 ~ 12/20/96
Jonathan Alexander Hancock ♥ 12/19/75 ~ 4/9/95
Jonathan Hall ♥ 5/2/83 ~ 12/23/10 and
Grandson ♥ 10/15/09 ~ 1/10/10
Jonathan Hunter Helwig ♥ 1/26/90 ~ 12/27/10
Jonathan Murillo Lopez ♥ 8/30/00 ~ 11/27/00
Jonathan T. Kormondy (J5) ♥ 3/17/71 ~ 12/10/10
Jonathan Wade Virden ♥ 5/4/89 ~ 10/4/12
Jonathen Brent Byrom ♥ 4/4/90 ~ 11/31/92
Jordan "Jordy" Walsh ♥ 1/14/98 ~ 3/2/07
Jordan Alexander Gallo ♥ 4/30/86
Jordan Avery Killian ♥ 11/19/93 ~ 8/13/07
Jordan Edward "Boomer" Mountjoy ♥ 4/21/90 ~ 4/30/07
Jordan Gregory Darrell ♥ 5/14/04 ~ 7/23/13
Jordan John Gose ♥ 6/15/87 ~ 6/12/10
Jordan Michael King ♥ 10/1/90 ~ 1/4/10
Jordan Paul Hacker ♥ 1/2/88 ~ 12/7/09
Jordan Sammy Rutherford ♥ 2/24/11
Jordyn M. Vaughn ♥ 10/13/99 ~ 6/25/04
Jose' Alfredo Colula Hernandez ♥ 7/28/09
Joseph "Joey" Anthony Gordon ♥ 11/22/81~ 6/19/02
Joseph Andrew Armstead ♥ 4/9/01 ~ 1/2/10
Joseph Anthony Scalise ♥ 11/02/90 ~ 6/22/09
Joseph Conner Weeks ♥ 9/22/93 ~ 10/16/13
Joseph Heverin ♥ 4/08/85 ~ 2/25/08
Joseph Michael Alkema ♥ 1/6/11 ~ 5/13/11
Joseph Paul King ♥ 11/29/87 ~ 3/26/10
Joseph Ryan Marino ♥ 9/6/93 ~ 8/13/09
Joseph Sewayah Ward ♥ 9/26/01
Joseph Tracy Baptista ♥ 10/18/99 ~ 3/30/07
Josephine "Josie" Francisco Herrera ♥ 9/1/91 ~ 10/13/10
Joshua " Boo Boo" Gage Pierson ♥ 9/28/08 ~ 4/29/10

Joshua "Dean" Hill ♥ 10/12/90 ~ 11/30/09
Joshua Angel Echelbarger ♥ 3/30/10 ~ 3/31/10
Joshua David Maitland ♥ 4/10/91 ~ 5/31/91
Joshua Eric Harrison ♥ 2/22/83 ~ 9/30/09
Joshua James Villatoro ♥ 12/18/10 ~ 3/27/11
Joshua Jay Farrar ♥ 3/13/82 ~ 3/11/04
Joshua Michael Barnfield ♥ 11/23/89 ~ 8/25/11
Joshua Paul Cope ♥ 7/25/79 ~ 8/12/00
Joshua Tyler Podsobinskin ♥ 3/21/93
Joshuajames M. Korczykowski ♥ 9/21/83 ~ 4/8/10
Julian Balboa ♥ 1/15/93 ~ 11/4/99
Julie Heather Hope Hall ♥ 2/20/76
July Marie Barrick ♥ 7/12/94 ~ 5/4/10
Justin Bice ♥ 9/16/88 ~ 3/8/08
Justin D. Burkhart ♥ 5/02/81 ~ 8/01/09
Justin Ellis Tidwell ♥ 10/8/91 ~ 7/20/09
Justin Fredrick Mitchell ♥ 6/30/82 ~ 3/21/07
Justin Hayes Wilson ♥ 8/8/01 ~ 5/21/10
Justin Jeffries ♥ 3/17/90 ~ 7/28/12
Justin Mark O'Meara ♥ 10/4/83 ~ 9/6/09
Justin Michael Gregg ♥ 12/03/85 ~ 10/4/10
Justin Ryan Maitland ♥ 8/22/80 ~ 10/7/80
Justin Seebeck ♥ 11/30/87 ~ 3/16/12
Justin Sherrill ♥ 10/25/90 ~ 04/26/12
Justin Stochmal ♥ 1/7/92 ~ 9/1/01
Justin Thomas Ward "JT" ♥ 3/29/89 ~ 5/2/13
Kaely "KK" Nicole Heaven Osterhus ♥ 8/29/05 ~ 4/17/09
Kaelyn Emilia-Hart Callender ♥ 1/14/09 ~ 5/21/10
Kaelyn Marie Rose Low ♥ 2/7/11 ~ 4/10/11
Kai Hartley ♥ 12/27/10
Kaidynce Leona Randolph ♥ 7/1/06
Kaila Marie Harlan ♥ 8/27/91 ~ 8/29/13
Kaili Marie Skeens ♥ 6/30/09 ~ 4/26/10
Kaitlyn Barbara Saenz ♥ 10/04/13
Kaitlyn Nicole Wingate ♥ 9/9/94 ~ 3/25/12
Kaleb Jordan Tutt ♥ 12/7/05
Kaleb Scott Lee Chidester ♥ 7/16/08
Kaleb Wayne ♥ 2/17/11 ~ 3/3/11
Kamberlyn Nicole ♥ 12/27/10

Kami Marie Tutt ♥ 9/23/09

Kamron Edwards ♥ 1/9/06 ~ 7/27/11

Kara Collins ♥ age 26 ~ 1/19/09

Karina Spaulonci ♥ 7/15/85 ~ 2/15/13

Karissa Marie Bermudez ♥ 11/9/08

Kasey Allen Swanger ♥ 2/05/82 ~ 12/18/05

Katelyn and Kristen Polson ♥ 11/30/95

Katey Lester ♥ 8/16/87 ~ 2/14/06

Kathlyn Joy Davis ♥ 7/30/09

Kathy Stiehl-Helms ♥ 1988

Katlyn Elizabeth Brewer ♥ 6/14/92 ~ 5/11/11

Katlynn Marie Smith ♥ 10/8/88

Katrina Diane Spinardi Moore ♥ 8/05/84 ~ 6/05/10

Katrina Moore ♥ 1/9/04

Keely Marie Devine ♥ 3/31/90 ~ 9/7/13

Kelli Marie Douglass ♥ 12/23/59 ~ 5/18/04

Kelly William Cheek ♥ 8/15/69 ~ 12/09/96.

Kelsey MacArthur Hanlan ♥ 5/14/85 ~ 4/14/07

Kelsey Tammy-Jo Norton ♥ 6/5/12

Kelsi-Dione Haffenden ♥ 5/11/01

Kenneth "KC" Hartman Conner ♥ 6/5/94 ~ 1/28/10

Kenneth Charles Russell II ♥ 7/19/83 ~ 1/8/11

Kenneth Jason Currey ♥ 11/5/75 ~ 11/29/99

Kenneth Lee Minks ♥ 8/7/85 ~ 8/26/09

Kenneth Moses ♥ 5/15/80 ~ 8/20/10

Kenneth Wayne McCormick III ♥ 6/24/89 ~ 7/6/12

Kenny Bowen ♥ 1/23/82 ~ 8/7/99.

Kenton Matthew Fults ♥ 11/12/08 ~ 4/1/10

Kerry-louise Bates ♥ 11/16/88 ~ 11/17/88

Kevin Anthony Sanders ♥ 8/09/95 ~ 11/22/10

Kevin F. Baker ♥ 1/7/78 ~ 7/12/05

Kevin Foster Hall ♥

Kevin James Davidson ♥ 8/8/97 ~ 8/3/98

Kevin Lee Crawford ♥ 8/18/89

Kevin Patrick Scullen ♥ 6/3/99

Kevin Thomas Bowles ♥ 2/10/71 ~ 4/4/91

Keyaera Anne Hughey ♥ 4/10/01 ~ 4/17/04

Kiana Sue Sommerville ♥ 12/8/08 ~ 2/24/09

Kieran William Shore ♥ 8/9/10 ~ 9/11/10

Kieren James Norris ♥ 5/10/93
Kimberly Marie Hamilton ♥ 8/14/87 ~ 5/7/04
Kirk Pfister Jr. ♥ 3/3/82 ~ 9/23/13
Kit Darwood ♥ 6/10/83 ~ 10/7/06
Korylette Kucken ♥ 6/29/00 ~ 6/1/11
Krista Leigh Dorsey ♥ 7/24/90 ~ 8/21/05
Kristen Marie Monzon ♥ 11/7/89 ~ 10/25/10
Kristi Hardin ♥ 4/5/93 ~ 4/28/11
Kristi Lee Landini ♥ 7/31/88 ~ 11/26/88
Kristie Lyn Hill ♥ 9/11/80 ~ 6/17/11
Kristy Sue Spicer-Spicer ♥ 3/9/73 ~ 4/5/11
Krystail Champain Yergeau ♥ 3/7/99 ~ 3/7/99
Kurtis Robert Cleaver ♥ 11/16/79 ~ 6/29/04
Kyle Barry John Rutherford ♥ 8/1/06
Kyle Jared Sullivan ♥ 4/29/88 ~ 10/20/09
Kyle Lloyd James ♥ 2/8/90 ~ 10/19/10
Kyle Richard Wene ♥ 6/16/86 ~ 2/8/11
Kyle W. Good ♥ 12/12/92 ~ 1/16 13
Kyran Alidar Liles ♥ 1/25/11 ~ 1/31/11
Landen Everett Epperson ♥ 1/01/99 ~ 9/12/10
Lane Clabough ♥ 2/11/00 ~ 1/24/13
Latesha Lee Mouser ♥ 4/05/88 ~ 1/1/10
Laura Lisa Bingley ♥ 11/23/87 ~ 9/15/08
Laura Lynne Wilson Wechsler ♥ 10/1/07 ~ 10/3/07
Lauren Elizabeth Pacenta ♥ 10/4/88 ~ 11/23/05
Lauren Lillian Robinson ♥ 9/22/10
Laurian Joy Baaske ♥ 2/23/97 ~ 7/04/10
Lawrence Wyatt Lee Fletcher ♥ 3/1/09 ~ 3/29/09
Leah Autumn Schaaf ♥ 9/14/05 ~ 5/1/08
Leeroy Damian De Leon ♥ 3/1/12 ~ 9/30/13
Leif Eric Harris ♥ 7/15/86 ~ 11/16/07
Leo Charles Oliver ♥ 1/30/13 ~ 8/28/13
Lexi Worrell ♥ 4/23/01 ~ 4/8/10
Lilianna Sofi a LaChangita ♥ 2/27/11
Lilyan Cayla Wilson ♥ 1/6/11 ~ 1/29/11
Lindsay Jean Wenzel Lopez ♥ 9/25/78 ~ 11/22/10
Lindsey Mae Maxwell ♥ 11/18/00 ~ 8/19/10
Lisa Elizabeth Goodwin ♥ 11/14/89 ~ 5/18/02
Lisa Jordan ♥ 2/2/74 ~ 5/27/09

Lisa Kay Holdgrafer ♥ 7/2/74 ~ 6/19/05

Lisa Marie Hammers ♥ 3/13/82 ~ 2/5/10

Lisa Michele Duran ♥ 11/26/71 ~ 8/19/07

Lisa Michelle Waring♥ 9/20/86 ~ 11/25/86

Logan Thomas Plant ♥ 6/1/04 ~ 11/17/10

Lorelai Tess Roberts ♥ 4/22/11

Luca Ortenzio ♥ 12/7/12 ~ 2/5/13

Lucas Damian Bortz ♥ 3/01/10 ~ 7/30/10

Lucas James Lafl eur ♥ 6/16/09

Lucas Richard Donnelly ♥ 6/3/11

Luke Howard Pendleton ♥ 7/06/10

Luke Hyslop ♥ 2/27/11 ♥ Angel and Whisper at 12 weeks

Luna Zola Beatty ♥ 4/15/03 ~ 4/16/03

Lydia Marie Greer ♥ 11/27/02 ~ 7/16/08

Lyra Jean' Mitchell ♥ 5/8/10

Macey Jaqeline-Rose Nind ♥ 4/18/11

Mackenzie Jones ♥ 8/22/02 ~ 8/26/02

Maddie Diane Kephart ♥ 2/20/88 ~ 4/29/11

Maddie Thomas ♥ 4/12/90 ~ 11/26/10

Madelyn Elise Buono ♥ 12/27/10

Madison Haley Arnold ♥ 10/01/94 ~ 3/12/09

Maggie Kovski ♥ 5/05 ~ 5/30/07

Maggie Mae Herrick ♥ 11/30/10

Malaikye Thomas Payne ♥ 3/29/10 ~ 8/15/11

Malaki Zane Mangum ♥ 11/20/99

Marc Kenneth Stanton ♥ 12/27/66 ~ 12/15/06

Marcus "Mark" Dean Tyler ♥ 4/19/66 ~ 12/5/92

Mareesa Abrahamson ♥ 4/22/72 ~ 3/01/11

Margaret Amelia Carey Kovski (Maggie) ♥ 5/6/05 ~ 5/30/07

Margaret Ruth Stewart ♥ 6/21/83

Maria Avalon Lovell ♥ 7/28/08 ~ 7/29/08

Marie Stockwell♥ 6/2/92 ~ 2/19/12

Marissa Nicole Olson ♥ 3/24/91 ~ 3/12/13

Mark Allen Gregory Jr. ♥ 1/22/05 ~ 8/13/05

Mark Anthony (Tony) Weber ♥ 6/13/95 ~ 11/27/09

Mark Harrison ♥ 3/10/82 ~ 12/10/11

Mark M. ♥ 11/14/78 ~ 4/3/03

Marley Skillman ♥ 9/25/09 ~ 12/17/10

Martha Rose Elliot ♥ 4/4/11

Marti LoMonaco ♥ 4/16/62 ~ 11/3/09
Mason Alexander Charles Eckhart ♥ 7/16/90 ~ 4/18/09
Mason Alexander Clink ♥ 7/9/11
Mason Jeremiah Wright ♥ 1/30/11
Mason Robert Diehl ♥ 10/18/13 ~ 10/19/13
Mathew Jameson ♥ 8/19/88 ~ 3/25/05
Mathew Wagner ♥ 3/1/94 ~ 7/15/04
Matt Tucker ♥ 12/7/82 ~ 11/19/08
Matthew ♥ 11/16/86 ~ 4/28/07
Matthew Broughton Garrett ♥ 11/20/78 ~ 10/9/10
Matthew Darren Bransden ♥ 2/13/81 ~ 10/12/81
Matthew David Herrera ♥ 5/19/88 ~ 11/10/09
Matthew Dean Hagan ♥ 5/24/85 ~ 4/4/03
Matthew Glenn DeSpain ♥ 6/25/89 ~ 12/13/91
Matthew H Witzgall ♥ 11/24/89 ~ 2/3/11
Matthew Keith Brashear ♥ 12/24/84 ~ 11/4/10
Matthew Liam Rupe ♥ 3/19/04 ~ 3/21/04
Matthew W. McKinnon ♥ 10/24/97 ~ 1/16/11
Maureen Chesebro ♥ 5/3/11
Maurem Marie Douglass ♥ 5/12/61 ~ 7/12/86
Maximus Allen Sevier ♥ 10/7/10 ~ 1/20/11
Meagan-Chante' Jacqualine Everton ♥ 12/8/99 ~ 11/2/11
Megan Ann Thornhill ♥ 3/7/90 ~ 1/28/13
Megan Lauren Major ♥ 2/23/80 ~ 3/8/11
Megan Mahan ♥ 12/04/01 ~ 3/29/13
Mekhail Isaak Mangum ♥ 5/24/00 ~ 6/4/00
Melanie Patricia Bourke ♥ 6/4/85 ~ 12/7/10
Melinda Rose Silva ♥ 5/13/76 ~ 1/6/05
Menetta Fenemor-Halsey ♥ 10/17/05
Merridith J Flick-Burke ♥ 2/16/77 ~ 10/18/01
Meshael Richardson ♥ 6/20/86 ~ 6/18/01
Micah Even Smith ♥ 5/27/07
Michael A. Crafton Jr. ♥ 7/15/04 ~ 8/3/04
Michael Alan Krack ♥ 8/11/99 ~ 6/4/00
Michael Bradley Baker ♥ 10/12/09
Michael D. Crotty ♥ 4/14/83 ~ 4/8/08
Michael Dwain Bradley ♥ 12/30/80 ~ 3/15/11
Michael Flynn ♥ 5/31/87 ~ 4/7/10
Michael Francis Limosani ♥ 12/06/88 ~ 10/26/09

Michael Jordan Svarc ♥ 10/20/84 ~ 4/01/11
Michael McKinley Royal ♥ 4/6/79 ~ 7/3/13
Michael Portaro ♥ 5/25/88 ~ 3/30/11
Michael R. Kern ♥ 4/30/81 ~ 4/13/07
Michael Reynolds ♥ 12/5/86 ~ 1/23/11
Michael Roy Anderson ♥ 10/16/90 ~ 10/17/10
Michael Serrett ♥ 8/21/84 ~ 6/20/10
Michael Steele ♥ 3/26/98 ~ 7/1/13
Michael W. Jackson ♥ 9/26/81 ~ 7/03/05
Micheal James Adkins ♥ 6/16/89 ~ 5/20/12
Micheal James Hammond ♥ 2/1/93 ~ 2/3/93
Micheal S. Wamser ♥ 5/11/87 ~ 12/17/10
Michelle Renee "Chelle" Walker ♥ 5/2/90 ~ 8/31/01
Michial Istre ♥ 6/2/79 ~ 9/2/06
Michial Istre Jr. ♥ 11/11/01 ~ 5/29/10
Mikey James Stokes ♥ 12/24/02 ~ 8/22/09
Mindy Christine Fohl ♥ 4/4/74 ~ 3/20/09
Miracle Faith Williams ♥ 8/17/11 ~ 8/18/11
Miranda Diane Daly ♥ 7/20/84 ~ 8/12/07
Miranda Lynae Boeckman ♥ 1/21/85 ~ 6/9/07
Miranda McFarland ♥ 2/18/89 ~ 2/25/89
Misha Stone ♥ 4/19/90 ~ 4/24/09
Mishale Anna Langston ♥ 9/17/92 ~ 12/6/92
Mitchell "Mitch" Scott Blank ♥ 10/15/66 ~ 7/27/01
Mitchell John Thomas Brennan ♥ 10/17/92 ~ 12/3/10
Monica Bivens ♥ 6/4/90 ~ 5/23/12
NaKeithan Scott Gray ♥ 3/6/10 ~ 5/4/10
Nancy Jane Prater ♥ 2/15/88 ~ 11/18/10
Narin Ramkumar ♥ 11/21/92 ~ 7/1/12
Natalia and Santiago Hernandez-Swain ♥ 8/07/09
Natalia Canales ♥ 5/14/11
Natalie Kathryn Johnson ♥ 3/30/98 ~ 12/1/09
Natallie Sue Kay Daugherty ♥ 6/10/11
Natasha Whitmore ♥ 1979 ~ 2007
Natassia Pereira Da Silva ♥ 8/1/83 ~ 8/29/07
Nathan Andrew Young ♥ 9/19/88 ~ 6/22/08
Nathan Bradley Lawrence ♥ 1/29/85 ~ 6/24/11
Nathan David Stratton ♥ 2/14/11 ~ 5/10/11
Nathan Lee Westberry ♥ 10/24/05

Nathaniel Matthew Payne ♥ 6/25/99 ~ 9/21/13

Naudia Fornfeist ♥ 12/27/10 ~ 2/12/11

Nayan Chandra ♥ 4/18/80 ~ 5/17/85

Naythan Maina ♥ 1/17/11

Nevaeh Hope Sousa ♥ 7/18/10 ~ 7/28/10

Nevaeh Neema ♥ 11/07/13 ~ 4/9/13

Niccolas Fogarty ♥ 7/8/91

Nicholas "Nic" Muir ♥ 6/25/87 ~ 4/13/07

Nicholas Alexander Arnold ♥ 6/26/01 ~ 11/7/02

Nicholas Isaiah Imler ♥ 7/29/76

Nicholas J. Marro III ♥ 8/31/82 ~ 10/9/10

Nicholas W. Swift (Nick) ♥ 9/29/93 ~ 8/15/12

Nicholas Wayne Steele ♥ 5/19/90 ~ 6/22/90

Nick Shelton ♥

Nickolas W. Eickenroth ♥ 6/2/88 ~ 8/10/05

Nicola Jane Perry ♥ 7/22/88 ~ 1/23/89

Nicole Byrd ♥ 3/28/93 ~ 8/19/96

Nicole Christine Bohlmeier ♥ 9/28/79 ~ 9/21/97

Nicole Marie Brown ♥ 3/28/89 ~ 1/1/07

Nicole Marie Klika ♥ 9/9/83 ~ 9/15/83

Nikolai Alexander McClain "Little Steven" ♥ 3/20/95 ~ 9/8/13

Nikolas Ryan Chunn ♥ 2/21/02 ~ 8/18/07

Noah Cooper French ♥ 7/15/11

Noah Fogarty ♥ 7/5/00

Noah Markiewicz ♥ 9/30/12 ~ 8/17/13

Noah Michael Mann ♥ 2/12/73 ~ 2/17/10

Nolan Michael Dowaliby ♥ 6/8/09 ~ 6/11/09

Nora Elizabeth Grothe ♥ 3/6/01

Nsuku Ndlovu ♥ 3/20/93 ~ 9/20/11

Ocean Rose ♥ 10/31/13

Oliver Murphy ♥ 4/18/11

Oliver Thompson ♥ 3/3/09 ~ 10/21/09

Oscar Charlie Oldfield-Archer ♥ 4/21/08

Osclie Oscar Oldfield-Archer ♥ 4/12/08

Owen Michael James Downes ♥ 1/15/01 ~ 6/2/01

Owen Walsh ♥ 6/12/10 ~ 6/13/10

P.J. Bueno ♥ 7/25/84 ~ 11/15/07

Paige Helen McCoy ♥ 4/1/08

Pamela Jolene Norman ♥ 4/24/80 ~ 3/2/06

Patricia "Trishie Bubbles" Ann Murray ♥ 4/7/84 ~ 7/12/10
Patrick "Charlie" Kelly Jr. ♥ 3/16/70 ~ 7/11/99
Patrick David Holley ♥ 2/14/81 ~ 2/13/10
Patrick Russell Caprino ♥ 2/20/69 ~ 10/20/12
Patrick Spencer Silbitzer ♥ 10/6/85 ~ 11/18/09
Patrisha (Trisha) Lee Ann Osipovitch ♥ 2/11/77 ~ 1/15/95
Patty Burgdoff ♥ 7/6/98 ~ 12/8/06
Paul G. Babloski Jr. ♥ 6/4/90 ~ 10/1/09
Paul Joseph Mithcell ♥ 9/29/47 ~ 2/23/69
Paul Wm. Schumacher ♥ 3/10/84 ~ 8/31/05
Pauline Michelle Craig ♥ 1/6/70 ~ 10/6/85
Philip Allan Walter Tognola ♥ 3/1/98 ~ 4/19/03
Phillip "PJ" Bueno Jr. ♥ 7/25/84 ~ 11/15/07
Phillip McFarland ♥ 8/18/93 ~ 11/5/12
Phillipa Campbell ♥ 11/3/89 ~ 8/28/09
Pip Connor ♥ 2/4/11
Poppy Ann Rudkin ♥ 7/11/10
Preston R. Madison ♥ 8/20/06 ~ 5/30/10
Princess Sienna Mary Rees ♥ 11/17/09
Priya Anjali Chandra ♥ 1/13/86 ~ 2/10/89
Quinton Liam Wallace ♥ 6/1/11
Rachael Ellen Thompson ♥ 11/5/81 ~ 6/26/08
Rachel Plog ♥ 4/18/90 ~ 12/8/06
Rain Serenity Arizola ♥ 10/20/07
Ramon M. Gallegos Jr. ♥ 11/24/80 ~ 11/27/10
Randi Mae ♥ 10/1/92 ~ 10/1/92
Randy Spurlock ♥ 5/3/71 ~ 1/10/11
Raymond A. Bryan IV ♥ 1/27/87 ~ 9/17/07
Raymond Benjamin Moppin Jr. ♥ 5/1/09 ~ 7/29/09
Rebecca and Rachel Tardif ♥ 3/11/04
Rebecca Anne Norris ♥ 10/10/79 ~ 9/12/09
Rebecca Louise Bosdyk ♥ 1/3/83
Rebecca Marie Peterson ♥ 7/6/89 ~ 9/30/07
Reed Alexander Cantler ♥ 10/23/96 ~ 12/22/10
Reed Joseph Kelsey ♥ 4/15/93 ~ 4/5/07
Ren and Simply ♥ 2/14/11
Rey of Hope Lucero ♥ 6/19/10
Ricardo E. Ignacio ♥ 1/8/87 ~ 7/9/07
Richard "Rick" Allen Fudge ♥ 1/3/84 ~ 10/24/85

Richard "Ricky" Scott Schumann ♥ 6/3/86 ~ 2/21/10
Richard Scott King ♥ 1/8/90 ~ 1/10/09
Richard Sylvester ♥ 11/1/85 ~ 11/1/06
Richard-John Alexander Akon Roberts ♥ 2/24/10
Ricky D. Lanham ♥ 9/21/79 ~ 12/23/10
Ricky Love ♥ 2/11/77 ~ 1/17/05
Ridgway "Ridge" Westin Blackburn ♥ 4/3/11
River Esparza Dougherty ♥ 4/27/98
Rob Niebieski ♥ 3/30/71 ~ 5/19/11
Robbie Gambrell ♥ 10/7/69 ~ 6/16/94
Robbie Mitchell ♥ 5/26/85 ~ 1/10/09
Robbie Robert David Speer ♥ 8/12/85 ~ 9/15/08
Robby Nelson ♥ 9/16/82 ~ 10/17/09
Robert "Bobby" Lee Kasch ♥ 7/17/80 ~ 5/19/06
Robert "Robbie" James Gambrel III ♥ 10/7/69 ~ 6/16/94
Robert Allen Hunt ♥ 4/14/86 ~ 1/16/11
Robert Fred (LB) Taylor ♥ 12/3/90 ~ 4/23/13
Robert Hanson Jr. ♥ 1/26/82 ~ 7/16/10
Robert John Clark II and Keith Raymond Clark ♥ 5/7/1972
Robert Joseph Cooper ♥ 4/12/73 ~ 5/30/95
Robert Layton ♥ 11/26/78 ~ 9/27/09
Robert Lee Hailes ♥ 4/2/88 ~ 7/12/06
Robert Mason Brewer ♥ 6/4/83 ~ 5/4/10.
Robert Raymond Huerta ♥ 9/29/76 ~ 7/7/00
Rocky Allan Lindley ♥ 8/28/83 ~ 10/19/07
Roger Dale Sanders ♥ 10/20/83 ~ 2/6/11
Roger Stiehl ♥ 2001
Rogerlee Staley II"BUBBY " ♥ 9/23/82 ~ 1/22/03
Roman Zac Craven-Phillips ♥ 5/3/09
Ronald "Ronnie" Allen Fraga ♥ 7/7/90 ~ 1/12/08
Ronald Landman ♥ 1/30/88 ~ 10/26/13
Ronnie Juett 3rd ♥ 3/14/84 ~ 9/7/05
Rory Lee Post ♥ 1/7/11 ~ 3/7/11
Russell Neil Coatsworth ♥ 10/25/81 ~ 6/10/09
Rusty Creepingbear ♥ 8/4/78 ~ 10/29/07
Rusty Hyitt ♥ 11/15/81 ~ 7/10/10
Ryan Andrew McGee ♥ 7/2/93 ~ 8/11/13
Ryan Blake Dunn ♥ 5/24/89 ~ 7/16/10
Ryan Dominic DeAndrea ♥ 7/22/82 ~ 3/16/05

Ryan Gene Johnson ♥ 6/16/13

Ryan James McPhee ♥ 10/6/83 ~ 7/8/10

Ryan Keith Harbuck ♥ 6/22/88 ~ 7/21/13

Ryan Michael Savidge ♥ 11/6/85 ~ 11/24/11

Ryan Nicholas Hunt ♥ 5/19/86 ~ 4/24/10

Ryland Cameron Stewart Swayze ♥ 6/9/07 ~ 5/20/10

Ryleigh Jade Karol ♥ 3/31/13

Ryleigh Jayne Wright ♥ 4/24/06

Salvatore Marchese ♥ 4/11/84 ~ 9/23/10

Sam Edward Garrison ♥ 8/29/10 ~ 3/22/11

Sam Moore ♥ 4/22/92 ~ 6/14/12

Samantha Downs ♥ 9/4/88 ~ 10/6/07

Samantha Lauren Martin ♥ 6/4/93 ~ 12/3/06

Samantha Lynn Puhr ♥ 5/24/90 ~ 11/11/11

Samantha Lynn Vogel ♥ 11/03/90 ~ 11/20/11

Samantha Rose Cleghorn ♥ 12/14/10

Sami Summers ♥ 11/16/79 ~ 3/19/99

Samira Joy Nukho ♥ 9/1/83 ~ 5/25/05

Samson Paul Lohaus Fast ♥ 10/15/10

Samual Thomas Smith ♥ 9/16/97 ~ 4/5/11

Samuel Watson ♥ 5/14/03 ~ 8/23/09

Samuel-John Wilson ♥ 1/4/10 ~ 9/4/10

Sara Brielle Knopick ♥ 6/25/08 ~ 8/8/08

Sara Elyse Eastley ♥ 10/7/87 ~ 10/8/10

Sarah E Kraemer ♥ 5/18/82 ~ 8/30/13

Sarah Elizabeth Logan ♥ 3/7/11

Sarah Lisa Guerrero ♥ 10/21/89 ~ 11/16/06

Sarah Natalia Salsano ♥ 11/19/05

Sarah Nichole Andricks ♥ 1/12/83 ~ 1/25/95

Sariah McKenzie Best ♥ 11/21/08 ~ 2/18/09

Savanah Marie Whitney ♥ 12/18/09 ~ 2/15/10

Savannah Elaine Berumen-Owens ♥ 5/24/11

Savannah Leigh Hart ♥ 4/4/94 ~ 1/19/97

Savannah Mahan ♥ 9/11/97 ~ 3/29/13

Scarlett Payne ♥ 1/3/09

Scarlette Adora ♥ 12/20/10 ~ 6/6/11

Scott A. Schwartz Jr. ♥ 9/2/85 ~ 4/20/07

Scott Allen Reece ♥ 3/8/73 ~ 8/5/10

Scott David Walz ♥ 9/12/91 ~ 3/4/10

Scott Duncan ♥ 8/5/79 ~ 4/12/09
Sean Alexander Turanicza ♥ 9/9/92 ~ 4/7/12
Sean Charles Grubbs ♥ 7/18/78 ~ 5/12/07
Serena Peyton Tasker ♥ 2/17/00 ~ 3/14/11
Serenity Grace Kushman ♥ 6/10/10
Sergio Hyland ♥ 5/28/02 ~ 8/6/04
Shannon Markiewicz ♥ 3/24/99 ~ 4/20/99
Sharonrose Gudu ♥ 7/2/12 ~ 10/19/12
Shaun David Hedstrom ♥ 11/14/81 ~ 5/11/13
Shawn Michael Broadus ♥ 6/5/87 ~ 4/11/06
Shawn Preston Rego ♥ 5/29/90 ~ 3/22/06
Shayla M. Aston ♥ 9/16/04 ~ 5/8/09
Shaylee Mikah Mangum ♥ 10/24/01
Shayna Alise Casilla ♥ 3/28/05
Shelbie Werth ♥ 10/5/94 ~ 6/6/11
Shelby Thomas McCorkle ♥ 8/27/00 ~ 3/6/11
Sheyenne Lynne Chappell ♥ 7/15/06
Shianna M. Aston ♥ 9/17/02 ~ 7/8/09
Sinead Morley-Shephard ♥ 7/12/06
Skyler DeShawn Bradley Priester ♥ 3/29/08 ~ 5/10/08
Sophee Olivia Widner ♥ 11/23/10 ~ 6/12/11
Sophia Grace Velazquez ♥ 5/31/11
Sophie Isabella Torrens ♥ 1/22/09 ~ 4/2/09
Spencer Matthew Jordan ♥ 9/30/05 ~ 10/25/05
Stacy Noel Sobieski ♥ 3/18/82 ~ 5/30/05
Stann Justice Davis ♥ 5/15/11
Stephen Anthony ♥ 2/15/11
Stephen Benjamin McClarence ♥ 4/23/87 ~ 2/6/89
Stephen Jon Ellenberger ♥ 7/16/91 ~ 4/1/08
Stephen LaSorsa ♥ 2/17/80 ~ 1/2/06
Stephen Tyler Dobbins ♥ 6/2/91 ~ 11/16/96
Sterling Snow Kushman ♥ 1/6/11
Steven Christopher Mills ♥ 9/15/92 ~ 5/22/10
Steven Eugene Handy II ♥ 2/3/02 ~ 7/18/02
Steven Lee Anglebrandt ♥ 12/27/87 ~ 7/23/07
Steven Lownie ♥ 5/30/84 ~ 10/7/07
Steven Mathis ♥ 1/31/74 ~ 5/15/04
Steven Michael Johnson ♥ 1/28/89 ~ 10/24/07
Steven Patrick Miller ♥ 8/31/84 ~ 3/31/06

Stewart Ian Reed ♥ 3/20/89 ~ 1/17/09

Sydney Anne Evans ♥ 10/19/07 ~ 11/28/09

Tabitha Renee' Drum ♥ 9/23/92 ~ 10/1/92

Tabitha Ruby Garay ♥ 12/31/01 ~ 7/9/12

Talia Rosaly Leombruno ♥ 10/18/10 ~ 2/07/11

Tamika Judith Short ♥ 12/3/95 ~ 12/5/05

Tammy Logan ♥ 9/17/90 ~ 2/5/91

Taylor Marie Vaughan ♥ 9/20/97 ~ 6/10/09

Taylor Noel Todora ♥ 1/15/87 ~ 6/18/07

Taylor Tropio ♥ 11/15/94 ~ 7/2/11

Taylor Vignes ♥ 1/15/87 ~ 6/18/07

Teagan Chloe Curtis ♥ 9/26/06 ~ 9/3/09

Teagan E. Dickenson ♥ 7/5/97 ~ 3/8/00

Teagan Eugene Paxton ♥ 9/20/06 ~ 11/26/06

Teara Renee Stokes Hagood ♥ 8/12/79 ~ 1/14/08

Tegan-Rose Major ♥ 5/31/07

Teresa Kay Lebo ♥ 9/13/06 ~ 3/17/07

Thomas Alan Losty ♥ 12/8/10

Thomas Joseph Ramsden ♥ 8/14/90 ~ 8/1/91

Thomas Joseph Serewicz Sr. ♥ 10/11/85 ~ 7/17/10

Thomas Lynn ♥ 8/31/02

Thomas Mathew Tucker ♥ 12/7/82 ~ 11/19/08

Thomas Wenzel Culver ♥ 9/6/75 ~ 6/26/02

Tiara Segrist ♥ 9/27/89 ~ 6/12/11

Tierra Rae Pierson ♥ 7/17/98 ~ 12/19/10

Tiffany Marie Gallo ♥ 3/23/87 ~ 6/25/11

Timmy Thompson ♥ 6/3/77 ~ 4/18/04

Timothy "Jason" Jones ♥ 5/24/09 ~ 10/31/09

Timothy Connors ♥ 7/26/95 ~ 5/17/11

Timothy E. Boutelle ♥ 5/10/89 ~ 7/28/10

Timothy Kyle Owens ♥ 10/24/77 ~ 6/24/11

Timothy Lee Nickos ♥ 6/12/94 ~ 6/28/11

Timothy Scott Hall ♥ 5/19/85 ~ 7/17/06

Timothy Thomas Moye ♥ 9/16/79 ~ 3/13/03

Tina Marie Elizabeth Gaither ♥ 9/20/95 ~ 11/10/98

Tina Michelle Lawson-Hutchens ♥ 2/25/83 ~ 4/24/03

Tiny Lux Lopez ♥ 3/9/10

Tomas Reece Morris-Welch ♥ 1/21/05

Tommy Bennett ♥ 9/18/99 ~ 11/25/03

Tommy Drake Randolph ♥ 8/24/07 ~ 4/28/08
Tommy Lee Baum ♥ 9/8/04 ~ 10/8/04
Tommy M. Childress ♥ 6/30/87 ~ 8/4/05
Toni Ann Hales ♥ 6/4/90 ~ 11/3/05
Tony Mahan ♥ 5/24/74 ~ 3/29/13
Tony Sansome ♥ 4/19/71~ 12/8/00
Tori Lee Cantu ♥ 2/17/97 ~ 4/14/10
Tracey Faye Pellegrini ♥ 10/27/74 ~ 1/11/08
Tracy Ann Gavel ♥ 1/25/74 ~ 10/9/88
Travis John Allen Carnes Sr. ♥ 12/19/86 ~ 12/5/12
Travis W. Mortimer ♥ 5/26/86 ~ 1/13/12
Trenton Cole Bailey-Stout ♥ 11/18/91 ~ 10/20/05
Trenton Lee Newlon ♥ 1/12/95 ~ 7/15/08
Trevor Wayne Jones ♥ 6/11/79 ~ 2/8/09
Treyton J. Whaley ♥ 9/24/06
Trinity Nicole Wright ♥ 1/11/10 ~ 2/22/10
Trisha Anne P. Dionisio ♥ 6/9/00 ~ 9/1/13
Ty Nichols ♥ 2/1/92 ~ 6/21/08
Ty Stevens ♥ 1/27/97 ~ 3/15/11
Tyler Boudreaux ♥ 7/28/89 ~ 4/16/09
Tyler Davis Lampman ♥ 7/27/96 ~ 10/19/09
Tyler Edward Dawdy ♥ 2/22/89 ~ 5/19/07
Tyler Paul Lippstreu ♥ 11/26/89 ~ 7/1/12
Tyler Ray Parmenter ♥ 9/4/72 ~ 3/30/02
Tyler Shane Richardson ♥ 8/14/04 ~10/3/06
Tyson Lee Shingledecker Coburn ♥ 7/7/10 ~ 3/14/11
Vallerina Jeanette Ramos ♥ 5/12/88 ~ 7/22/88
Veronica Jane Oulch ♥ 5/7/81 ~ 10/2/11
Vicky Leanne Johnson ♥ 8/31/03
Vito E. Pistone IV ♥ 10/22/81 ~ 7/10/10
Walter Timothy Cohen ll ♥ 8/14/89 ~ 1/25/10
Warren V. White ♥ 1/24/03 ~ 4/23/11
Waylon Andrew McDonald ♥ 10/2/81 ~ 10/14/12
Wendy Sunderlin ♥ 6/18/77 ~ 11/12/96
Wesley Dustin Imler Sr. ♥ 6/3/77 ~ 8/29/05
Wesley Hunter Yackle ♥ 8/05/03 ~ 6/03/06
Wesley Wayne Phillips ♥ 3/10/81 ~ 7/23/08
William "Billy" King ♥ 12/14/90 ~ 11/9/08
William David Hawkins♥ 3/20/02

William Durasky ♥ 4/30/87 ~ 12/2/12
William Gaines Lowe ♥ 7/27/10
William Hart ♥ 5/2/07
William James Sansalone ♥ 5/24/95 ~ 7/29/05
William M. Harkanson ♥ 10/30/85 ~ 2/23/88
William Mullis (Daniel) ♥ 8/17/89 ~ 5/13/12
William S. Carney ♥ 7/17/80 ~ 6/5/04
Willow Kyliegh Loralye Chapman ♥ 1/22/11
Wyatt Dillon Caviglia ♥ 12/28/08 ~ 2/2/11
Wyatt Miracle Lee ♥ 12/9/07 ~ 4/7/08
Xandrea Jolean Cruz ♥ 9/10/02 ~ 10/11/02
Xavier Michael King ♥ 1/27/98 ~ 6/6/11
Xavier Ricky-Allan Tanswell ♥ 11/16/10
Xzavier Alan Francisco ♥ 4/14/03 ~ 5/29/11
Yasovardhan Thakur ♥ 4/25/90 ~ 12/15/11
Zachariah Dennis Marsh ♥ 8/27/95 ~ 10/5/07
Zachariah Moore ♥ 7/13/08 ~ 7/25/08
Zachary Aaron Smith ♥ 3/20/82 ~ 6/18/03
Zachary Allen Thacker ♥ 2/25/86 ~ 9/23/10
Zachary Bynum ♥ 10/17/94 ~ 1/7/13
Zachary Devon Shafer ♥ 2/19/08 ~ 12/8/08
Zachary James Cook ♥ 7/2/92 ~ 11/8/09
Zachery Murdock ♥ 3/3/96 ~ 2/2/13
Zachry Thomas Patrician ♥ 9/1/95 ~ 8/25/13
Zackary Matthew Bell ♥ 1/12/01 ~ 6/13/01
Zahra Belle Benboubaddi ♥ 6/28/11
Zakk Anthony Devlin ♥ 8/11/09
Zane Reagan Draycott ♥ 1/06
Zina Ann Manuel Pitts ♥ 11/14/63 ~ 11/2/13
Zineb Beatrice Benboubaddi ♥ 6/29/11
Zoe Ann Lawhon ♥ 5/6/11 ~ 5/6/11
Zoe Isabella Lemmons ♥ 10/31/10
Zoe Maree Wait ♥ 2/23/81 ~ 7/26/04
Zoey Mae Rea ♥ 6/21/12
Zoey Rae-Leigh Hawkins ♥ 3/11/03
Zoey Renee Elizabeth Lin Smith ♥ 12/29/01 ~ 4/12/04
Zoie Nina Woods ♥ 11/9/10

Epilogue by J. T. Baptista

You did it! You completed this workbook and are learning to connect to the other side. I have been working with my mom for six years and I am so happy to be able to work with you now. Yes, I am working with you! For everyone who reads this workbook and follows the weekly exercises, I am available if you need assistance. Call me in as you do your automatic writing or during your meditations and I will be there. Don't be surprised if I show up as someone older than when I left. You see, I can be any age I want. Sometimes I like to be a teenager and sometimes I like to be in my twenties. My energy is the same regardless of how old I appear, so be assured that it will be me.

So what do you want to do next with this? Where do you see yourself in the next month? Year? What does your future hold for you? You know, with the skills you have learned and are continuing to learn, you now have control back of your life. You are the co-creator of your reality and with this comes some responsibility. You can no longer just let life happen. You can grab it by the horns and direct it where you want it to go. What does that look like for you?

Seven years ago when I left, my mom did not know if she would ever be able to smile again. Her life was simply about surviving. Maybe some of you are like that now, too. My mom learned and you can too, that this is not how it has to be. Even if you have lost a child (by the way, we really aren't lost, but that's what my mom says about it, so that's what I will write here) you can have joy again. My mom isn't special in this way. She is very special in many ways but she will tell you just like I am that anyone can get their life back no matter what the circumstances. What we here in heaven want for all of you is to be able to love and experience joy and life again, no matter what. In six years' time, my mom found what she needed to move the grief out and bring the joy in. Does that mean she doesn't miss me? No, of course not. But it means we have a different relationship and whenever she starts going down that grief path, I stop her and tell her she doesn't need to do it that way anymore. I am here and I am not going anywhere.

Your angels, guides and loved ones are the same. They want the best for you, including joy. Don't feel that just because my mom has clear connection that it's not the same for you. Because you should know by now, you have clear connection too…or you are getting there. Don't give up! Don't look back. We are right here to help you continue your training—all of your loved ones angels and guides, and me. And don't think you are bothering us, because we love to help! It is why we are here! So what does this all mean for you? Are you ready to put aside the existence you have now for a brand new one? One with life and love and joy? Then don't stop connecting with us, and don't ever think you are on this road alone. I wish you could see how many of us are around you right now, all with your highest good and best intention for you. Trust me. It's amazing.

If you didn't guess by now, my mom is ready to help you, too. You can ask her about her long distance connecting training if you want, and it's a great way to get your guides involved. I help her with all of her students, so you will definitely be seeing more of me.

Let's see, what else do I want to say? That you are loved beyond your wildest dreams. No matter what has happened in your life to this point, we love you. All of us. Bring that into your heart and feel it. We will never leave you, either. No matter what the appearance of your life, it is an illusion. We are always here with you. Bring that into your heart, too.

Now it's your turn. Meditate and get clear and then decide where you go from here. I can promise you an experience of a lifetime if you let it come to you. What do you say? You want to fly with us or not?

About The Author

Sarina Baptista is an internationally renowned psychic medium, mentor, author and speaker. She was a featured speaker for the "Life, Death and Beyond" International Conference in Crete, Greece, and is the resident psychic for Clear Channel's Big Country 97.9FM in Northern Colorado. Her clients include adults and children from all areas of the world, including Australia, Italy, India and the UK. Her purpose is to connect us to our angels, guides and loved ones, and teach us how to access this information on our own.

Sarina discovered her gifts through her own tragedy—the passing of her seven-year-old son in March 2007. She learned her son did not really die. He was still very close, leading her to her incredible mediumship gifts. Knowing her son is happy and close by whenever she calls to him made such a difference in her grief recovery.

Sarina works with a collective of Ascended Masters who can see what her clients need and assists in each session. She has created several mediumship training programs, including one on one mentoring, long distance training, workshops and webinars to train others to connect with the other side based upon what she has learned from her son and the Ascended Masters. She holds monthly live events and development workshops demonstrating how we are all connected.

Sarina is also the Psychic Investigator Team Lead for Third Eye Paranormal Investigators, a Northern Colorado paranormal team, and educates home and business owners about these "residents" in their space.

She currently resides in Loveland, Colorado, with her husband, three children, dog and cats. J.T. calls her work "The Bridge to Healing: Connecting Heart and Soul."

For more information about Sarina, please visit http://www.sarinabaptista.com.

Resources

Recommended Reading

Baptista, Sarina A Bridge to Healing: J.T.'s Story – A Mother's Grief Journey and Return to Hope. Bloomington: Balboa Press 2013

Choquette, Sonia Ask Your Guides. Carlsbad: Hay House, 2006.

Holland, John Power of the Soul: Inside Wisdom for an Outside World. Carlsbad: Hay House, 2008.

Newton, Michael Ph.D. Journey of Souls: Case Studies of Life Between Lives. Woodbury:Llewellyn Publications, 1994.

Van Praagh, James Growing Up In Heaven. New York: HarperCollins, 2011.

Weiss, Brian, MD. Many Lives, Many Masters. New York: Simon and Schuster, Inc., 1988.

Websites

http://www.sarinabaptista.com
My website has grief information, resources and more information on how to connect with your loved ones, angels and guides

http://www.johnholland.com/
John Holland's website has very valuable information on mediumship. His weekly newsletter is also full of great information and tips to tapping into your psychic self.

Meditation CDs

Bridge to Healing Connecting Meditations available at www.sarinabaptista.com

Meditation: Achieving Inner Peace and Tranquility In Your Life — a book with a CD by Brian Weiss, M.D.

Connecting with Your Animal Spirit Guide — by Steven Farmer

Psychic Navigator: Harnessing Your Inner Guidance — a book with a CD by John Holland

Made in the USA
San Bernardino, CA
06 April 2015